Protozoa and the water industry

Colin R Curds DSc

Keeper of Zoology
The Natural History Museum
London

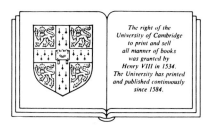

The right of the University of Cambridge to print and sell all manner of books was granted by Henry VIII in 1534. The University has printed and published continuously since 1584.

CAMBRIDGE UNIVERSITY PRESS

Cambridge
New York   Port Chester   Melbourne   Sydney

Published by the Press Syndicate of the University of Cambridge
The Pitt Building, Trumpington Street, Cambridge CB2 1RP
40 West 20th Street, New York, NY 10011–4211, USA
10 Stamford Road, Oakleigh, Victoria 3166, Australia

First published 1992

Printed in Great Britain at the University Press, Cambridge

A catalogue record for this book is available from the British Library.

ISBN 0 521 39731 6 paperback

Cover photograph: *Euglena Spirogyra* showing pellicle
© Biophoto Associates

Contents

Introduction

Protozoa are single-celled, microscopic organisms of various forms. They are famous – perhaps infamous would be a better word – as agents of disease and death, but most protozoa are not harmful and this book attempts to redress the balance. Although there are large numbers of parasitic protozoa there are far more free-living species inhabiting all types of aquatic and terrestrial habitats. Many of these play a vital and useful role in our everyday lives without our even being aware of their presence. For example, protozoa form a vital link in many food chains in fresh and marine waters and are of real economic significance in the prevention of organic pollution of those habitats. Furthermore, they can be used to monitor the operation of sewage-treatment processes and to indicate the degree of organic pollution affecting flowing waters.

It is only within the past three decades that biologists have turned their attention from the medical and veterinary aspects of protozoology to the ecology of free-living protozoa. This has resulted in a new awareness of their great importance in many habitats. This book discusses the importance of free-living protozoa in fresh waters and, in particular, their role in helping us to maintain good quality water supplies and control pollution.

In the first chapter the general problems of water supply and pollution are discussed with some background information on how one can define and measure pollution. The second chapter sets out to introduce the reader to protozoa and, in particular, those found associated with polluted waters. Chapter 3 discusses the subject of organic pollution and how it affects protozoa and certain other organisms.

The next two chapters explain fully the processes used to produce good quality drinking water and purify organic waste waters. Two chapters follow on the role played by protozoa in water and waste-water treatment and how mathematical models can help to explain their significance.

The final chapter considers the parasitic protozoa that are transmitted in contaminated waters causing public health problems. Examples include *Entamoeba histolytica*, the causative organism of amoebic dysentery; *Naegleria fowleri*, the amoeba responsible for amoebic meningitis; the flagellate *Giardia intestinalis*, which causes gastric problems (known as 'hikers' disease' in North America); and a newcomer on the scene, the coccidian parasite *Cryptosporidium muris*, which has recently caused several deaths in AIDS patients. Also reviewed in the final chapter is the recent discovery that the bacterium *Legionella*, the causative organism of Legionnaire's disease, can live and multiply inside free-living freshwater protozoa. This is an exciting new development, the full implications of which are yet to be appreciated.

1

Water, water supply and pollution

Supply and demand

To anyone who has seen satellite pictures of the planet earth, surely the most impressive feature is the apparent abundance of water. This immense quantity of water, covering 71 per cent of the earth's surface to a mean depth of 3.8 km, measures in volume about 1.4×10^9 km^3. This water has been derived over geological time from the water present in the magmatic rocks that formed the earth some 5000 million years ago. Today, however, it takes many forms in the biosphere – the surface region of the earth where living organisms exist.

Table 1.1 provides an inventory of the waters in the biosphere and an indication of the time taken to replenish them. The first point to notice is that while water is indeed plentiful on earth, water fit for immediate human use is not. Only a maximum of about 0.3 per cent of the world's total water resources is available for human usage. The second point is that groundwater, by far the largest useable water resource, and fresh-water lakes, have relatively long renewal periods when compared to rivers and atmospheric water vapour. These latter have short renewal times but only contribute about 0.3 per cent to the total useable water supply.

The ultimate source of fresh water to replenish rivers, lakes and groundwater is rainfall. If it were evenly distributed over the entire land surface it would correspond to a precipitation of 72 cm per annum. The problem is that rainfall is not evenly distributed, nor is it all available to us. About one-third of the precipitation that falls on land is returned to the oceans as river flow. The other two-thirds is returned to the atmosphere by evaporation from exposed water surfaces and as a result of plant transpiration. Only the river-flow part is actually available for human use and this is roughly equal to 37 500 km^3 per annum.

Table 1.1. *Inventory of water in the biosphere, modified after Kalinin and Bykov (1969)*

Water resource	Percentage of total	Renewal time
Oceans	97.61	37 000 years
Polar ice and glaciers	2.08	16 000 years
Groundwater	0.29	300 years
Freshwater lakes	0.009	1–100 years
Saline lakes	0.008	10–1000 years
Soil and subsoil moisture	0.005	280 days
Rivers	0.00009	12–20 days
Atmospheric water vapour	0.0009	9 days

When this volume of water is divided by the earth's human population (4000 million) it appears some 25 000 litres per day are available per head. Comparing this figure with the human physiological requirements for water of about 2 litres per person per day, these values seem immense. Even when the actual useage of water is taken into account (e.g. 40–250 litres per day per head for domestic purposes, up to 1500 litres per head per day for industrial consumption in technologically developed countries and up to several thousand litres per head per day for agriculture in countries with hot, dry climates) there is still an apparent huge surplus of available water.

Why is it then that so many countries have growing water supply problems? Even Canada, which has 9 per cent of the world's river flow and only 0.7 per cent of its population, has problems. There are many reasons but the major ones are these. Firstly, the world's population is not distributed over the earth's surface in proportion to rainfall or river flow. Secondly, supply problems typically develop during periods of low flow in hot, dry weather. Thirdly, demand for consumption has risen with increased availability and standard of living. Finally, pollution lowers the quality of water, thereby reducing the supply for certain purposes. In the poorer developing countries such problems are acerbated by the needs of expanding populations and their ability to pay for the materials and expertise required to deal with them.

Water supply and treatment processes

The increased demand for water has resulted in the need to plan, manage and integrate the supply, use and treatment of water to a much greater extent than before. In less demanding times towns could rely upon the proximity of natural, unpolluted water sources that could be simply filtered, used, purified and the effluent discharged to the sea via a river – probably the one from which the water was taken.

Unpolluted water sources are now less likely to be nearby. They are likely to be many miles away in remote purpose-built reservoirs. Thus rivers carrying effluent have to be used as sources which require more and more complex and expensive methods to treat both **effluents** and **abstracted water**. Frequently on a major river, one town's effluent has become another's raw water supply.

The processes used to treat water for drinking purposes differ markedly from those used to treat sewage and industrial wastes, although there are many similarities in the biological processes that are employed as will be seen in later chapters. Fig 1.1 represents the geographical and physical relationships between the sources, uses and processes employed by the water industry to obtain and treat water and effluents. Water for drinking purposes is obtained from a source that is as free from pollution as is possible. Sources may include groundwaters, catchment areas with lakes or reservoirs, or rivers. Waters from such sources are abstracted for storage in a reservoir before some form of treatment that will ensure that the water is of a sufficiently high standard for human consumption. Water of such quality is known as **potable water** and it is distributed to towns and cities through underground pipes to be used for domestic and industrial purposes, although some major industries may have their own source of lower quality water for industrial usage only.

Once used, the water is transported to a sewage-treatment works where a combination of physical, chemical and biological methods are employed to ensure that the effluent has as little polluting effect upon the receiving water body as is economically possible.

What do we mean by pollution?

Up to this point, the word 'pollution' has been used without definition. In fact it is not easy to give an all-embracing definition for this commonly used term. To many members of the general public pollution implies the introduction of something dirty, unclean or unpalatable into the environment, regardless of the amount or effects of the materials introduced. This idea of pollution does not easily include the introduction of small amounts of radioactive materials or toxic substances or the causing of temperature or salinity changes. Thus I prefer to rely upon Martin Holdgate's (1980) definition of pollution:

> 'The introduction by man into the environment of substances or energy liable to cause hazards to human health, harm to living resources and ecological systems, damage to structures or amenity, or interference with legitimate uses of the environment'

He further paraphrased this definition more simply as being:

> 'something in the wrong place at the wrong time in the wrong quantity'

Holdgate stresses that while his definition is only a superficial generalisation, it does retain the basic essentials that pollution is caused by substances or energy, that the location of the pollutant and its effect in space and time are crucial and that a judgement about what is acceptable or not is

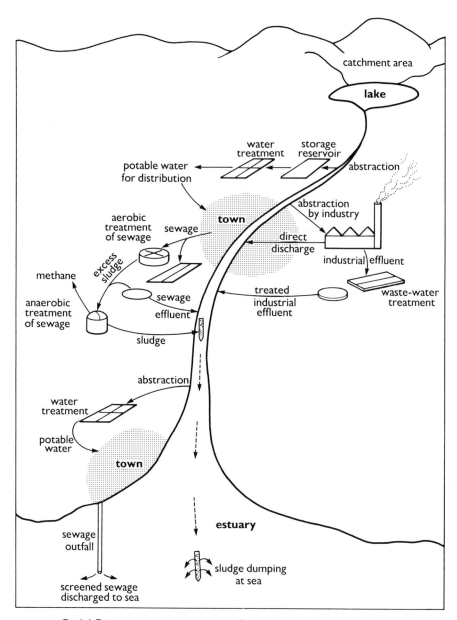

Fig 1.1 Diagrammatic representation of common sites of water and sewage-treatment processes in the UK.

inevitable. Pollution is brought about by human activities and involves the interactions of them with the natural world. Thus as Holdgate points out:

'pollution has to be evaluated in a socio-economic context which is why there is so much argument about it'

Pollution comes in many forms. It can be energy based (heat, sound, nuclear, etc) or substance based (sewage, heavy metals, pesticides, etc.) and can be classified in a variety of different ways – by its nature, properties, the sector of the environment it affects (air, sea, fresh waters, land), by its source and in several other ways. The interested reader is recommended to consult Holdgate's stimulating review of the complex nature of pollution and its effects upon organisms and the environment.

For our purposes here we shall use the terms 'pollution' and 'pollutant' in a highly restricted way. We are mainly concerned with water-borne organic pollutants, both soluble and particulate, and their effects upon populations of certain organisms in fresh waters. The source of pollution we consider most frequently is domestic sewage derived primarily from human body and kitchen wastes. However, it should be pointed out that in most towns throughout the world sewage will inevitably contain a proportion of waste waters derived from industry and it is neither possible nor wise to totally ignore the presence of these substances.

How do we measure pollution?

Pollution can be measured in two totally different ways – either by estimating the concentration of a specific pollutant or pollutants or by estimating its effect upon the environment. Members of the public usually have to rely upon the second method, which is unfortunate since by the time the visual effects are obvious the problem has become extensive. However, water authorities and other monitoring bodies use both approaches in their efforts to prevent or reduce pollution. An outline of how organic pollution can be measured chemically is given below, followed by a discussion of the chemical and physical effects of organic pollution upon fresh waters.

Measurement of pollutant concentration

Sewage and sewage effluents are the major sources of organic pollution in the world. Certain industries, such as the food industry, also contribute to the organic pollutional load but in minor amounts when compared to those produced by households.

The polluting strength of sewage or sewage effluent is assessed by the use of various analytical procedures, including the five-day **biochemical oxygen demand (BOD_5)**, **chemical oxygen demand (COD)**, **total organic carbon (TOC)**, **suspended solids (SS)** and **ammonia** concentrations. The first three of these tests attempt to assess the concentration of organic matter present and the likely effect of the polluting liquid upon the dissolved oxygen concentration of the receiving watercourse. None of the three give the total picture and their results are not always necessarily directly related to each other. However, each analysis does give information that the others do not and for this reason several tests are usually performed on each sample. Each test or analysis is briefly outlined and discussed below.

Biochemical oxygen demand   When polluting organic matter is discharged into a watercourse, natural purification immediately begins due to the action of micro-organisms, particularly bacteria. These organisms utilise the atmospheric oxygen dissolved in the water to oxidise the polluting substances present. The length of time required for complete purification to take place depends upon many factors, including temperature and the nature of the organic matter.

The **Royal Commission on Sewage Disposal** proposed that the weight of dissolved oxygen required by a specific volume of liquid for the process of biochemical oxidation during a period of five days at a temperature of 20°C be taken as a measure of the quality of the liquid. This test was first known as the dissolved oxygen absorption test but is now almost exclusively known as the **biochemical oxygen demand**, usually abbreviated to **BOD** or **BOD$_5$**. The five-day period was chosen because it was the average retention time of a British river. The analysis is simple but arbitrary; the dissolved oxygen content of the liquid, with or without dilution, is determined before and after incubation for five days at the standard temperature, the difference giving the oxygen demand of the sample.

Although simple in principle, the test is difficult to interpret and it has been criticised for many years. However, it has been used as a standard for an equally long period of time and, provided the standard procedures are adhered to, it can be used for comparative purposes on similar effluents as a useful indicator of the pollutional load. On domestic sewage and effluents the BOD$_5$ test provides a useful indication of comparative strengths since they contain suitable bacterial populations and varied bacterial foodstuffs (or substrates). For other types of effluents it may be less satisfactory for a variety of reasons. Industrial effluents, for example, may contain bactericidal substances which inhibit or prevent biological oxidation except at high dilutions, or they may contain insufficient bacteria. However, even when used to assess effluents such as sewage, the BOD$_5$ test has one major disadvantage – the results are not available until five days after sampling. This can be a major handicap to sewage-works operators who wish to monitor the performance of the plants they are operating and also to chemists who wish to detect pollution quickly so that appropriate action may be taken promptly.

Chemical oxygen demand   The time delay problem of the BOD$_5$ test was partly responsible for the introduction of other methods aimed at assessing the oxygen demand – methods which could be measured rapidly, and chemically rather than microbiologically. Originally the chemical oxidising agent chosen was potassium permanganate. Results could be obtained in about four hours, but it was later found out that the method did not give complete oxidation and suffered from interference by certain other chemicals present (nitrites and high chloride concentrations). Although this test, known as the four-hour permanganate value, was used in Britain for many years it eventually gave way to the **chemical oxygen demand** test (**COD**) which uses potassium dichromate as the oxidising agent and had found increasing favour in the USA. The COD dichromate method involves boiling the sample with potassium dichromate and 50% sulphuric acid for two hours. This results in a more complete oxidation and with many organic wastes was found to give results very similar to those obtained with the BOD_5 test. In many cases once the BOD:COD ratio has been established for a particular waste, the COD test can replace the BOD_5 test for rough control in routine work.

Total organic carbon As both the above-mentioned analytical methods are aimed, at least indirectly, at assessing the concentration of organic matter present in an effluent, one could ask why the direct determination of the total amount of organic matter present would not give a more reliable result. There are several reasons for this. Initially there were technical difficulties in estimation which have since been overcome and it is now relatively simple to carry out a **total organic carbon** (**TOC**) analysis if the equipment is available. However, the way in which the carbon is combined is important. For example, phenol and glucose exert different oxygen demands because the sugar molecule contains slightly more oxygen in its structure than phenol. Furthermore, not all carbon sources are biodegradable. For example, a suspension of cellulose would not be detected by a BOD_5 test, nor would oxalic acid. They would be detected by an organic carbon analysis or by a chemical oxygen demand test. For these reasons most workers continue to determine all three parameters – BOD_5, COD and TOC – so that they can assess their own situation more fully and obtain data that can be compared to those of others.

Suspended solids Suspended solids in sewage range in size from the gross to the colloidal; the former are generally removed by physical means at the sewage works before biological treatment takes place. The remaining liquid is often called **settled sewage**.

Whatever form of biological treatment is used to treat the settled sewage, the effluent will be settled again before its discharge to a watercourse. Settling will depend on the rate of sedimentation which depends upon several factors, one of the most important being the size of particles. Under normal circumstances, at least at sewage works situated on inland sites, only the smallest particles remain in suspension. Thus a high concentration of effluent suspended solids would indicate a pollution problem of some description.

Particles suspended in sewage effluents are usually organic in nature, biodegradable, and therefore exert an oxygen demand which can be detected by the BOD_5 and COD tests. Non-organic particles from sources other than sewage will present different problems depending upon their constitution.

Micro-organisms form a significant proportion of the particulate matter borne in sewage and sewage effluents. They include viruses, bacteria, fungi and protozoa. Those in sewage originate from faeces, soil and water. Sewage effluents have, additionally, those micro-organisms actually growing in the biological-treatment plant itself. These may be radically different to those entering in the sewage.

There is typically 12–30 mg l^{-1} (milligrams per litre) dry weight of bacteria suspended in sewage. More than 70 distinct pathogenic human viruses have been detected in sewage, most commonly including those which cause polio and gastric problems. The protozoan fauna of sewage has been studied less but, certainly, flagellates such as *Bodo* spp. are common, as are amoebae and certain ciliates.

The **suspended solids concentration**, together with the BOD$_5$ and the ammonia concentration, help to define what is known as a **Royal Commission standard effluent**. This indicates that the effluent conforms to a 20:20:30 standard, which means it contains concentrations equal to, or less than, 20 mg l^{-1} BOD$_5$, 20 mg l^{-1} ammonia and 30 mg l^{-1} suspended solids.

Nitrogenous compounds   Ammonia arises as a rule from the aerobic or anaerobic decomposition of nitrogenous organic matter and, if detected in a watercourse in quantities of above 0.2 mg l^{-1}, would strongly indicate the presence of sewage or sewage effluent. Ammonia and ammonium compounds are toxic to fish even in relatively small amounts. The toxicity is affected by the pH value (toxicity increases with pH) and by the concentration of dissolved oxygen present (toxicity decreases with increase in dissolved oxygen).

The average British domestic sewage contains about 46 mg l^{-1} ammonia. In sewage works, this ammonia is oxidised in two stages by two different autotrophic bacteria, first to nitrite by *Nitrosomonas* and then the nitrite to nitrate by *Nitrobacter*. The overall process is known as **nitrification**. The degree of nitrification achieved is often used by sewage-works operators as an indicator of the overall performance of the plant, since total nitrification only occurs when optimal conditions for the breakdown of organic material are satisfied.

Composition of sewage   The main source of pollution in sewage is human excreta, with smaller contributions from food preparation, washing, laundry, surface drainage, etc. A typical industrial waste, which can also be part of sewage, consists of one or more strong waste liquids from the main industrial process together with comparatively weak waste water from rinsing, washing, condensing, floor-washing, etc. The major components of industrial waste depend on the nature of the industry producing the effluent and they are therefore highly variable in composition. On the other hand, the composition of domestic sewage is, qualitatively, far more consistent from one town to another and even one country to another.

Remarkably few investigators have actually studied the composition of sewage in any detail and most information has been gathered from individuals interested in specific compounds. What is known shows that the composition of sewage *in toto* is far from static. Changes are known to occur in the flow, strength and composition of sewage – hourly, daily and seasonally. Of these the hourly variations are usually the greatest. Variations in flow are normally inversely proportional to the size of the community served. The hourly variation is normally 50–200% of the average but can be wider. Strength and composition also vary considerably during a complete day. A fairly regular pattern of strength reaching a peak at noon and a trough at about 5 p.m. is normal.

Sewage treatment

In countries like Britain two main methods are used for the treatment of sewage and industrial wastes. The older method uses bacterial beds, which are also known as percolating or trickling filters. Settled sewage is dosed, usually by means of rotating distributor arms, at a steady rate over beds of clinker. A slime accumulates on the surfaces of the clinker which supports large populations of bacteria, fungi, algae, and protozoa as well as many macro-invertebrate animals. These break down the sewage and purify the water. They were used for many years as the major method for the treatment of waste waters but eventually lack of space, especially in big cities, became a problem.

In 1914 this situation led Dr G.J. Fowler of the University of Manchester, in co-operation with E. Ardern and W.T. Lockett of the Manchester City Council, to devise the activated-sludge process. This new process produced, on average, a far superior effluent to that of percolating or biological filters and needed much less space. The activated-sludge process operates by dosing a steady flow of settled sewage into an aeration tank which is kept aerobic by the bubbles of air introduced through diffuser domes. A sludge consisting of colloidal material, bacteria and protozoa develops and, after approximately eight hours' aeration, is removed from the effluent by sedimentation in a settling tank. A small proportion of the sludge is removed for disposal but the majority is returned to the aeration tank to be mixed with the flow of settled sewage. This process is still one of the most widespread methods in use today.

Effluent is not the only product of a sewage-treatment works; large amounts of biological solids or sludge are also produced and these are usually dumped at sea, although currently there are many pressures to stop this practice.

Organic pollution and self-purification

On entry into a river most of the organic compounds (proteins, fats, carbohydrates, etc.) in sewage and sewage effluents can be broken down by microbial action with an accompanying consumption of dissolved oxygen. Even some toxic organic compounds such as phenol can be degraded in this way provided the toxin is in sufficiently low concentrations. Such substances are said to be **biodegradable** or biologically 'soft'. However, certain other organic compounds, such as cellulose, lignins, hydrocarbons, many synthetic pesticides and most of the original 'hard' synthetic detergents that were developed in the 1950s, are highly resistant to microbial decomposition, and these substances will remain in the environment, accumulating, for long periods of time. These are the biologically 'hard' compounds which, because they are either totally non-biodegradable or highly resistant, are not accompanied by an oxygen demand.

If the organic pollutional load is small, consisting mainly of biologically 'soft' compounds and diluted by a sufficiently well-oxygenated body of receiving water, then aerobic bacteria will be able to break down the organic matter completely to relatively harmless, stable and odourless end-products, such as carbon dioxide, water, nitrates, sulphates and phosphates. The body of water therefore recovers naturally from the organic pollution and is said to have undergone self-purification. However, only too frequently heavy organic pollution results in the growth of large populations of bacteria which quickly exhaust the supply of dissolved oxygen. The remaining organic material is then broken down by anaerobic bacteria which do not require free oxygen but can utilise the oxygen combined in the form of nitrates, phosphates, sulphates and organic compounds. Anaerobic fermentation occurs, resulting in a different and noxious set of end-products such as methane, ammonia, amines, hydrogen sulphide and phosphine, many of which have objectional odours. A river that is anaerobic is often said to be 'dead' or 'lifeless', but the use of such descriptions should be avoided; they are certainly not lifeless since they contain anaerobic bacteria and protozoa, but equally they do not support fish or most of the invertebrates that one would find in an unpolluted, aerobic river.

The rate at which self-purification can take place depends upon many factors, including the original dissolved oxygen concentration of the river water, the amount and kind of organic pollutant, the dilution factor and the rate at which oxygen enters the system. This means that chemical, physical and biological factors are important in the control of self-purification. The most obvious effect of organic pollution on the chemistry of a river is the associated decrease in the concentration of dissolved oxygen. This is illustrated in fig 1.2 where the idealised effects of three different levels of organic pollution on the dissolved oxygen concentration of a river are shown. It will be seen that light organic pollution produces a

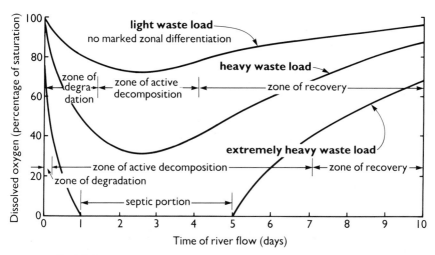

Fig 1.2 Oxygen sag curves for three rivers receiving organic loadings of increasing concentration.

shallow depression in the dissolved oxygen concentration, which quickly recovers after self-purification is complete. The depression is usually called the **oxygen sag** and is caused by the respiratory rate of the micro-organisms being greater than the rate at which oxygen can enter the system. In this first case the river remains aerobic and as soon as the organic materials have been utilised, the aerobic microbial growth and respiratory rates decrease to such an extent that the rate of reaeration becomes greater. This allows the dissolved oxygen concentration to return to its original, unpolluted level.

In the second example, the heavy organic pollutional load produces a much greater oxygen sag. The river remains aerobic but return to the unpolluted condition takes place much further downstream. In the third case, where the pollutional load is extremely heavy, the river actually becomes anaerobic. Aerobic self-purification ceases and water quality worsens. However, eventually aerobic conditions return downstream and the dissolved oxygen concentration recovers. The anaerobic phase will have a disastrous effect upon the fauna and flora of the river with all aerobic life being eliminated from that stretch and for a considerable distance downstream.

The factors controlling the dissolved oxygen concentration of an organically polluted river interact with each other but can be divided into two main groups – those which control oxygen consumption and those which control reaeration. Both main groups comprise a mixture of physical, chemical and biological factors which are discussed below.

Oxygen consumption   Microbial populations consume dissolved oxygen when growing aerobically upon organic substrates. Thus the factors controlling oxygen consumption are those which control growth and respiration. These include temperature; the warmer the water, within reasonable limits, the greater are growth and respiratory rates and hence oxygen consumption.

The nature and concentration of the organic pollutant is also very important. Substances easily utilised by micro-organisms will quickly exert an oxygen demand while other, non-biodegradable substances will not be utilised. The concentration of utilisable substances (substrate) controls the growth rate of micro-organisms so dilution by the receiving water is also important. A high substrate concentration will induce high microbial growth and respiration rates and will result in a high population of organisms. All these factors will stimulate a high oxygen demand.

Reaeration   The rate at which oxygen is replenished – reaeration – is controlled not only by several river variables, including flow rate, turbulence and water depth, but also by the amount of photosynthesis taking place. All these factors interact with weather conditions. The addition of fresh, well-oxygenated water from tributaries downstream can also greatly influence reaeration.

The physical characteristics of the river and nature of the bed are important factors in reaeration. In fact any factor increasing turbulence will increase reaeration and, hence, self-purification. The introduction of physical devices such as weirs will greatly increase reaeration. During the restoration of water quality in the River Thames in London, mechanical aerators were sometimes used to offset the organic load discharged by certain industries until a more permanent method of waste disposal could be introduced. Indeed, it has been suggested that oxygen injection barges be set up on the Thames as an emergency treatment to combat accidental organic spills and storms which increase oxygen demand.

The introduction of biologically 'hard' detergents in the 1950s caused many rivers to be covered in blankets of foam, often several feet high. The foam was unsightly and tended to be blown about by the wind but this problem was minor compared to the deleterious effect upon reaeration of the watercourse. The foam covered the air–water interface and prevented the diffusion of oxygen into the water, with catastrophic results. Fortunately, the introduction of biologically 'soft' detergents in the 1960s solved the problem completely.

All plants containing chlorophyll fix atmospheric or dissolved carbon dioxide in the presence of sunlight and water with the release of gaseous oxygen. They also respire aerobically using oxygen and releasing carbon dioxide. The rate of respiration can be measured during the night and it is assumed that respiration takes place at the same rate during the day. The release of gaseous oxygen into the surrounding water has a profound effect and large diurnal fluctuations in the dissolved oxygen concentration of river water have been noted by several workers. Photosynthesis, of course, depends on the amount of available sunlight, among other factors, but it can be a potent influence on reaeration. The input of oxygen via photosynthetic plants is used in some sewage-treatment processes such as waste stabilisation lagoons (see page 62) where algae keep the process aerobic.

Sewage effluent can be an excellent source of nitrates, particularly when the treatment plant is working sufficiently well for nitrification to take place. Nitrates can be removed by further biological treatment known as denitrification or by chemical means. Phosphates, derived mainly from household detergents, are also present in appreciable concentrations. These two chemicals are plant nutrients and their concentration, at least partially, controls the biomass of water plants grown, particularly algal populations when sufficient sunlight is available. However, sewage-treatment works also tend to produce suspended solids which can appear in the effluent and when severe these can deplete or eradicate water plants in rivers by smothering them and reducing light penetration.

In lakes where the input of nitrates and phosphates is significant, heavy blooms of green algae and blue-green algae may result, a phenomenon known as **eutrophication**. When the bloom dies it will rot by microbial action, causing oxygen depletion of the surrounding water and the release of toxic substances. Both of these effects have been implicated in the death of fishes following algal blooms. Eutrophication tends to be a major and long-lasting problem in lakes, which takes many years to recover even after the input of nutrients has been stopped.

Nitrates, also, are a potential hazard when present in high concentrations in drinking water. For many years they have been known to cause a disease in infants known as methaemoglobinaemia where water containing $10\text{--}20 \text{ mg l}^{-1}$ nitrate has been used in the preparation of baby milk. Recent studies link high nitrate intake, forming nitrosamines in the gut, with certain cancers in animals.

2

Protozoa – the organisms

'Protozoa' means 'first-animals' and they are still defined in some traditional textbooks as simple, microscopic, single-celled or acellular animals. However, it is now recognised that protozoa are not simple, not necessarily single celled, certainly not acellular, and perhaps should not be regarded as animals. The organisms commonly referred to as protozoa include a diverse assemblage of nucleated micro-organisms that were fitted into a single phylum of animals. More modern classifications, however, divide living things into four or more kingdoms and perhaps the most widely used scheme is the five-kingdom classification – Monera, Protista, Plantae, Fungi and Animalia. In such a scheme the protozoa can be considered as a subkingdom of the kingdom Protista. In each case, the former major groups of Protozoa would become phyla.

An introduction to the Protozoa

In common with all other micro-organisms, protists possess the attributes of both cells and entire organisms. As cells they are eukaryotic, that is to say they have a nucleus bounded by a nuclear envelope, and are elaborately differentiated by a series of membrane systems. In comparison, prokaryotic cells such as bacteria are much simpler in their construction and do not contain membrane systems.

As entire organisms, protozoa are capable of reproduction, feeding, movement, excretion, respiration and sensitivity. Most protozoa reproduce by binary fission involving a mitotic division of the nucleus, but sexual processes are widespread in several groups. A variety of nutrition and locomotory mechanisms are found among the protozoa but all have to perform these complex physiological processes within the confines of a specific microscopic size. The majority of protozoa are within the size range of 5 and 250 μm in diameter, although foraminifera are often larger and the exceptional *Stannophyllum* attains a diameter of several centimetres.

The first protozoa were seen by Antony van Leeuwenhoek in 1674 and, at present, more than 65 000 protozoan species have been described. Protozoa are found in all moist habitats. Although many may survive arid conditions by the formation of a resistant cyst, none can feed in the absence of water. Thus protozoa are common in the sea, soil and fresh waters; and examples of parasitic protozoa are found in most animal groups.

Some protozoa have solved the problem of living in a changing environment by becoming adaptable in their morphology or nutrition. For example, the soil amoeba *Naegleria* secretes a resistant cyst to prevent desiccation during dry weather, is a naked amoeba in moist soils, but produces flagella when flooded with water.

The distribution of cysts in the atmosphere and of trophic forms in the seas and fresh waters has resulted in a more or less cosmopolitan spread of free-living species throughout the world. However, the geographical distribution of higher-animal hosts and some human activities (such as land-drainage schemes and the use of insecticides to reduce the incidence of invertebrate hosts) means that many parasitic species have a restricted distribution pattern.

Certain parasitic protozoa are of great medical and veterinary importance. For example, *Plasmodium* is responsible for the disease malaria, while *Trypanosoma* spp. causes sleeping sickness in Africa and Chaga's disease in South America. In domestic animals *Trypanosoma brucei* causes the disease nagana in cattle, and *Eimeria* coccidiosis in rabbits and poultry. Free-living protozoa are equally important, especially in ecology. The **autotrophic** forms are primary producers at the base of most food chains. Similarly the predatory activities of the **holozoic** protozoa provide the vital link in the food chain between the heterotrophic bacteria, many invertebrates and subsequently vertebrates.

Classification of the Protozoa

It is evident from what has been said above that it is not possible to make an all-embracing definition of the Protozoa. The classical classification of the Protozoa proposed at the turn of the century considered them to be a single phylum containing the Mastigophora, Sarcodina and Sporozoa in one subphylum and Ciliophora in another. This scheme was largely based on locomotory organelles and was still in use in 1964 when the Society of Protozoologists published its first classification. The classification outlined in table 2.1 is adapted from that Society's most recent version; it is not intended to be complete, but all major groups are included and some examples of protozoa mentioned in this book are given. It can be used as a guide to the next section which provides an introduction to the structure, physiology and reproduction of some major examples of protozoa.

Mastigophora and Sarcodina – the Sarcomastigines

Sarcomastigines comprise those protozoa usually referred to as flagellates, amoebae, foraminifera, heliozoa and radiolaria. It is a diverse group of protozoa with the common feature of possessing flagella and/or

Table 2.1. *Abbreviated classification of the subkingdom Protozoa, giving some examples of those found associated with polluted waters*

Phylum 1 Sarcomastigophora
Flagella and/or pseudopodia present, spores not produced

Subphylum
1 Mastigophora. Flagella typically present, division by longitudinal binary fission.

Class
1 Phytomastigophorea. Plant-like flagellates typically with chloroplasts; if missing, relationship to pigmented forms clearly evident. e.g. *Euglena* and *Peranema*.

Class
2 Zoomasitigophorea. Animal-like flagellates. Chloroplasts absent, one to many flagella, amoeboid forms, with or without flagella. Many parasitic forms. e.g. *Bodo*, and *Giardia*.

Subphylum
2 Opalinata. Binary fission takes place between rows of cilia which cover the entire body in oblique rows; two or many monomorphic nuclei. All parasitic. None associated with polluted waters.

Subphylum
3 Sarcodina. Pseudopodia typical, flagella restricted to developmental stages when present.

Superclass
1 Rhizopoda. Locomotion by pseudopodia or by protoplasmic flow without production of discrete pseudopodia. Includes the naked (*Acanthamoeba*, *Amoeba*, *Entamoeba* and *Naegleria*) and testate amoebae (*Arcella*, *Euglypha*), the foraminifera and the slime-mould amoebae.

2 Actinopoda. Spherical, typically planktonic. Axopodia with delicate internal microtubular skeleton. Some naked, others with tests of chitin, silica or strontium sulphate. e.g. *Actinophrys*.

Phylum 2 Apicomplexa
Apical complex visible with electron microscope. All species parasitic.

Class
1 Perkinsea. No sexual reproduction, incomplete cone. None in polluted waters.

Class
2 Sporozoea. Sexual and asexual reproduction typical; oocysts generally containing infective sporozoites which result from sporogony. Locomotion of mature organisms by gliding. Includes the gregarines and coccidia. e.g. *Cryptosporidium*.

Phylum 3 Microspora
Unicellular spores each with imperforate wall, containing one uninucleate or dinucleate sporoplasm. Always with polar tube and cap. Obligatory intracellular parasites in nearly all major animal groups.

Table 2.1. (*cont.*)

Phylum 4 Ciliophora
Cilia or compound ciliary organelles present in at least one stage of life cycle. Two types of nucleus present; sexual and asexual reproduction. Plane of division transverse across ciliary rows.

Class
1 Kinetofragminophorea. Oral cilia only slightly distinct from body ciliature. Cytostome often apical or mid-ventral on surface of body. Body ciliation commonly uniform. e.g. *Acineta, Amphileptus, Chilodonella, Colpoda* and *Litonotus*.

Class
2 Oligohymenophorea. Oral apparatus, at least partially in buccal cavity, generally well defined, although absent in one group. Oral ciliation clearly distinct from body cilia. Cytostome usually ventral at or near anterior end at bottom of a buccal cavity. e.g. *Carchesium, Colpidium, Glaucoma, Paramecium, Uronema* and *Vorticella*.

Class
3 Polyhymenophorea. Dominated by well-developed, conspicuous adoral zone of numerous buccal or peristomial ciliary organelles. Cytostome at bottom of buccal cavity. e.g. *Aspidisca, Euplotes* and *Metopus*.

pseudopodia. It contains three subphyla, although one of these, the Opalinata, is not represented in the environments covered by the present book.

Mastigophora The flagellated protozoa (fig 2.1) all possess long whip-like organelles, the flagella, which are used mainly for locomotion. The presence of pseudopodia is not uncommon in flagellates and this chapter serves to demonstrate their close affinities with the amoebae and other rhizopods. All flagellates reproduce asexually by longitudinal binary fission, that is to say the plane of division lies along the major body axis.

The plant-like flagellates typically have chlorophyll-bearing plastids called chloroplasts, though this is not always the case. Nevertheless, in those examples where chloroplasts are absent, there is an obvious and close relationship between them and the pigmented forms. Most of these flagellates, like plants, fix atmospheric carbon in the presence of sunlight and have an **autotrophic** mode of nutrition. However, few are completely autotrophic. Many that are photosynthetic are also known to be able to grow in the dark using organic carbon sources such as acetate and are therefore capable of **heterotrophic** nutrition. It should not be forgotten that oxygen is one of the products of photosynthesis and this is important in certain sewage-treatment processes such as oxidation ponds (see chapter 5) where photosynthetic protist populations are used to keep the process aerobic. In fact a wide range of nutritional types are exhibited by the plant-like flagellates (fig 2.1) and in one order, the Euglenida, examples of

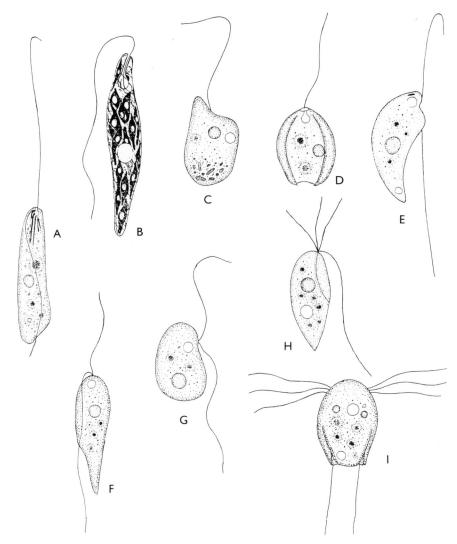

Fig. 2.1 Some flagellates commonly found in sewage-treatment processes.
A–D are phytoflagellates: A *Peranema trichophorum*, B *Euglena gracilis*,
C *Oicomonas termo*, D *Nostrosolenus orbicularis*. E–I are zooflagellates:
E *Bodo caudatus*, F *Cercobodo longicauda*, G *Pleuromonas jaculans*,
H *Tetramitus decissus*, I *Hexamitus inflata*.

autotrophy (*Euglena*), heterotrophy (some *Euglena* spp. and *Astasia*) and
phagotrophy (*Peranema*) are to be found.

   None of the animal-like flagellates possess chloroplasts and they are not
closely related to any that do. They are heterotrophs with a marked and
widespread tendency towards parasitism and commensalism and few lie
within the scope of this book. Some of the simpler forms with few flagella,
such as *Bodo* (fig 2.1E), are common in organically enriched waters of all
types while *Giardia*, one of the more complex forms with duplicated

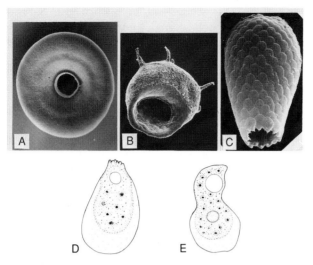

Fig 2.2 Some naked and testate amoebae commonly found in sewage-treatment processes. A–C are shells of testate amoebae: A *Arcella vulgaris*, B *Centropyxis* sp., C *Euglypha* sp. D–E Naked amoebae: D *Vahlkampfia vahlkampfi*, E *Amoeba guttula*.

organelles, is a human pathogen responsible for alimentary disorders and is transmitted in contaminated waters.

Sarcodina   The subphylum Sarcodina is divided into two superclasses, the Rhizopoda and the Actinopoda. The rhizopods comprise the well-known naked amoebae which may be either free-living or parasitic. The free-living forms which occur in polluted waters include both the naked amoebae and the testate amoebae (fig 2.2). The latter have well-developed shells or tests with a single orifice from which the pseudopodia project. The tests may be an organic secretion as in *Arcella*, constructed of siliceous plates as in *Euglypha* or built from inorganic debris derived from other organisms (e.g. diatom frustules) and inorganic sources in the local environment (e.g. sand grains) as with *Difflugia*. All of the free-living forms are phagotrophic heterotrophs. These feed on other micro-organisms including bacteria, algae and other protozoa by engulfing them with their pseudopodia. Parasitic examples include *Entamoeba histolytica* the dysentery amoeba, *Naegleria fowleri* the amoeba responsible for amoebic meningitis, and *Acanthamoeba* spp. which cause similar conditions. The dysentery amoeba is transmitted in polluted water while *Naegleria* and *Acanthamoeba* are transmitted in waters which are not necessarily polluted.

Asexual binary fission is the normal method of reproduction in amoebae. However, sexual reproduction is widespread in the foraminifera, another large rhizopod group. These have calcareous shells perforated by many holes through which a network of pseudopodia extrude. The vast majority of foraminifera are limited to marine and estuarine waters and no examples have been reported from polluted fresh waters.

The Actinopoda form the second superclass of the Sarcodina and include the radiolarians and heliozoans. The former is a wholly marine group with complex siliceous skeletons. Several heliozoa are found in fresh waters and one species, *Actinophrys sol*, has been detected in biological filter effluents. *Actinophrys*, in common with most heliozoa, is spherical in shape and covered with radiating, spine-like pseudopodia. The actinopods are supported and stiffened internally by sheaths of microtubules which are temporary structures like other pseudopodia. They may also be used to engulf prey as do the pseudopodia of amoebae.

The Apicomplexa

This phylum was established in an attempt to make some sense of the heterogeneous assemblage of parasitic protozoa often referred to in earlier texts as the 'Sporozoa'. That name was inappropriate since 'spores' are not present in many members of the group. All species in the phylum are parasitic, and some are extremely important as agents of disease such as malaria, still the most important human disease, and coccidiosis and piroplasms which cause heavy losses in domestic animals.

The coccidian genus *Cryptosporidium* is the only member of the Apicomplexa known to be associated with contaminated waters. It was first observed in the laboratory mouse early in the twentieth century but, as it was not known to be of any particular importance, was almost totally ignored for the next 60 years except by taxonomists. Then it was discovered to cause diarrhoea in young calves and subsequently in humans. The first cases of human cryptosporodiosis were reported in 1976 but relatively few were subsequently diagnosed until it was found to be a life-threatening infection in acquired immune deficiency syndrome (AIDS).

The Ciliates

The ciliated protozoa possess several features in common indicating that they are a truly natural group. All possess cilia at some stage in their life cycle. Cilia are used for both locomotion and feeding. They often cover the body in parallel longitudinal rows and beat in an apparently co-ordinated fashion known as metachronal rhythm. In some ciliates, the cilia may be bound together to form compound organelles known as cirri, and in the crawling hypotrichs these take the form of stout, leg-like structures upon which the organism walks.

Cilia are also commonly used for feeding and are often grouped together to form undulating membranes and membranelles. The former are composed of a single line or arc of cilia fused together along their length, and the latter are formed by blocks of several rows of fused cilia. These specialised feeding organelles beat strongly to produce a vortex current of water bearing particulate food flowing towards the oral region. Most ciliates have a single, well-defined oral area in which food particles are collected before being engulfed into a food vacuole. The food is digested

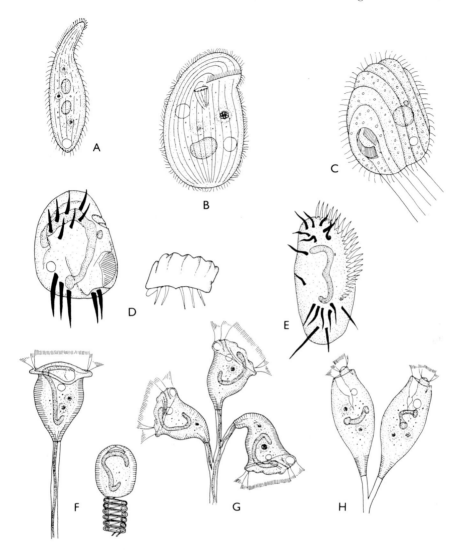

Fig 2.3 Some ciliates commonly found in sewage-treatment processes.
A *Trachelophyllum pusillum*, B *Chilodonella uncinata*, C *Cinetochilum margaritaceum*, D *Aspidisca cicada* (vental and rear views), E *Euplotes affinis*, F *Vorticella convallaria* (extended and contracted), G *Carchesium polypinum*, H *Opercularia coarctata*.

inside this vacuole by various enzymes which are released from lysosomes which fuse with the vacuole. Undigested remains are discharged to the exterior via a permanent pore. Excess water is expelled by the pulsating action of one or more transparent vacuoles known as contractile vacuoles. Most ciliates feed upon other micro-organisms such as bacteria, fungi, algae and protozoa, including other ciliates.

Many ciliates (fig 2.3) swim freely in water but some, such as the peritrichs and suctoria, are attached to surfaces, such as those of plants or organic debris, sometimes by means of a stalk. The suctorians and some peritrichs such as *Vorticella* are solitary, but several peritrich genera such as *Epistylis*, *Carchesium*, *Zoothamnium* and *Opercularia* are colonial and are borne upon branching stalks which may be contractile or non-contractile. The sedentary life style introduces certain problems not faced by those ciliates swimming freely in the water. For example, a change in the local environmental conditions, such as lack of food, becomes a real problem to a sedentary ciliate. In *Vorticella*, this has been solved by developing an ability to grow a ring of aboral cilia, break free from its stalk and swim to a site with better prevailing conditions.

Ciliates have two kinds of nucleus. The much larger macronucleus is the vegetative or trophic nucleus, concerned with the day-to-day running of the cell. The micronucleus is very much smaller than the macronucleus. It is the generative nucleus and is concerned with sexual processes. A ciliate can often survive indefinitely without a micronucleus. Indeed several amicronucleate strains of ciliates have already survived in laboratories for several decades. However, the presence of a macronucleus is vital to the ciliate's survival.

Most ciliates reproduce both asexually and sexually. Asexual reproduction is the normal method of increasing numbers of a species and sexual processes ensure the transfer of genetic material from one individual to another, so increasing the variety of individuals in a population.

Asexual reproduction in ciliates is usually by binary fission which takes place transversely across the major body axis and at right angles to the ciliary rows. Conjugation – the temporary joining of two individuals – is the usual method of sexual reproduction. Mating can occur only when two mating types (i.e. sexes) of the same species mix together. Usually the sexes are similar in form and structure. Their differences are essentially physiological.

The majority of ciliated protozoa are free-living but there are some exceptions. One major group, the Astomata, are found in the blood cavity (haemocoele) of invertebrate animals; *Ichthyopthyrius* causes white spot disease in fishes and some *Tetrahymena* species are parasites of invertebrate animals. Certain specialised anaerobic ciliates inhabit the rumen of herbivorous animals where they ferment certain plant materials. They form large populations which are later digested. Available evidence suggests that ruminants containing ciliates grow faster than those without them. Only one ciliate, *Balantidium coli*, can be said to be a human parasite, and as such it is uncommon. It is primarily a parasite of pigs.

Ciliates are very common in organically polluted waters of all types. Most ciliates are aerobic, but some specialised free-living ones are strict anaerobes and are limited to anaerobic environments which require a high input of biodegradable organic matter.

Organically enriched waters support very large populations of bacteria upon which ciliates feed. Large numbers of ciliates may be found in sewage-treatment processes where their rapid growth and feeding rates ensure that they play an important role in the removal of suspended bacterial populations from effluents.

3

Biological effects of organic pollution

Overall effects

Before focusing our attention upon the effects of organic pollution on aquatic protozoa we need first to consider its impact upon the overall chemistry and biology of a watercourse. Studies in many countries on the biology of rivers polluted by a wide range of organic pollutants have shown that, although there are important differences in detail, broadly similar effects occur. These are illustrated in fig 3.1. Many of the biological changes noted may be related to the drastic reduction in dissolved oxygen concentration. However, it should be remembered that sewage and sewage effluents contain not only dissolved organic matter but also suspended solids, poisons such as ammonia and sulphides, inorganic nutrients and other constituents. These may interact with each other and it is often difficult to match cause with effect.

The main overall ecological effects of organic effluents in rivers are to change the existing biological communities in terms of both species content and abundance. For example, the reduction in dissolved oxygen concentration will eliminate those species which cannot live under such conditions, enabling others, which can, to replace them. However, since fewer organisms are able to withstand polluted conditions, the number of surviving species tends to decrease, that is to say species diversity is reduced. Conversely, the addition of greater concentrations of organic and inorganic nutrients will increase the total biomass of organisms above that which would be supported by the unpolluted watercourse. Such an organically polluted river tends to produce a greater biomass of fewer, and usually different, species when compared to the same river in its unpolluted state.

If you examine part A of fig 3.1 you will see that following organic

23

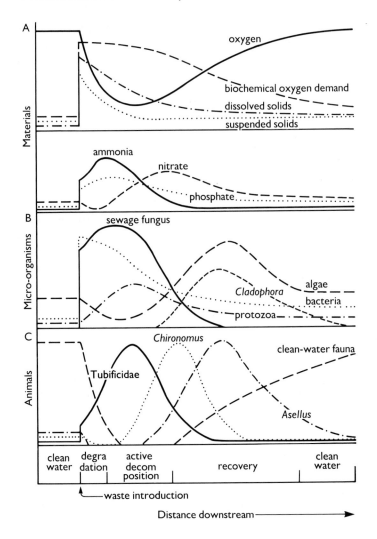

Fig 3.1 Typical changes in the water quality and animal and plant populations of a river as it passes through various zones following the introduction of sewage. After Bartsch (1948).

pollution, changes occur down the length of the river as it undergoes self-purification. The dissolved oxygen concentration is at first depressed, displaying the well-known oxygen sag (see fig 1.2, page 11). Further downstream the river's oxygen content returns to its original level as the soluble and suspended organic pollutants are oxidised. The example in fig 3.1 illustrates a case of fairly severe pollution, though not so severe as to totally deplete the dissolved oxygen concentration. As one might expect, the BOD_5 of the river water rises sharply at the source of pollution but, as self-purification proceeds, this declines slowly towards its original value. The amount of suspended solids rises initially but quickly falls, partly due to sedimentation and partly to being broken up by oxidation processes. The ammonia concentration rises initially and continues to rise as the organic nitrogenous wastes are degraded but, as soon as nitrification sets in, the ammonia concentration decreases and the nitrate level rises.

Specific changes: bacteria

Sewage contains very large populations of bacteria, particularly those of faecal origin, and, although over 90 per cent of these are removed during biological sewage-treatment processes, they are still present in sewage effluent in concentrations of about 1×10^6 ml^{-1}. In fact quite high populations of bacteria are present in most organic effluents which grow on the organic matter in a river when they enter it. However, the species which grow in the river are unlikely to be the enteric faecal coliform bacteria borne in the sewage but other species more suitable to life in river waters. A lot of time-consuming effort is necessary to identify bacteria and this has resulted in less information on changes in river bacterial populations than on most other groups of organisms. However, there are many surveys which include total and viable bacteria counts in the data collected. These indicate that most organic effluents are a good source of bacteria. Even if the effluents are sterile, the river water which they enter is itself an abundant source. Whatever their origins, the bacteria will inevitably grow on the organic substrates. However, as it proceeds downstream the substrate becomes depleted, predation of the bacteria by protozoa begins and the bacterial population decreases.

Specific changes: the sewage fungus community

Profuse growth of what is called 'sewage fungus' is a common sight in an organically polluted river. The title 'sewage fungus' is a misnomer since it is not usually fungus. It is far more likely to consist mainly of the filamentous bacterium *Sphaerotilus natans*, although a variety of organisms including some fungi may also be present. The term 'sewage fungus' is used to describe the presence of filamentous or slime-like growths visible to the naked eye which are frequently associated with organically polluted rivers. The term has no taxonomic implications. In the UK about 75 per cent of outbreaks of sewage fungus extend for less than 1 km downstream of the point where organic pollutants are discharged, although 1 per cent extend for more than 8 km. Most outbreaks are associated with domestic sewage discharges, although some industrial effluents, particularly those from distilleries, fruit and vegetable canning, and paper manufacturing, are also important. Detailed surveys have revealed that the major constituents of sewage fungus in the UK include a great variety of bacteria, fungi, algae and protozoa. Table 3.1 lists the organisms most frequently found. *Sphaerotilus natans* and zoogloeal bacteria are by far the most common slime-forming organisms. They are found in 89 and 93 per cent of sites respectively and form the major part of the total biomass at 50 and 59 per

Table 3.1. *Organisms most frequently found in sewage fungus growths in the UK. After Curtis and Curds (1971)*

Organism	Percentage occurrence
Bacteria	
Zoogloeal bacteria	93.4
Sphaerotilus natans	88.9
Flavobacterium sp.	36.9
Beggiatoa alba	29.6
Flexibacterium sp.	25.2
Spirillum sp.	13.4
Blue-green 'algae'	
Oscillatoria spp.	5.6
Phormidium sp.	4.5
Fungi	
Geotrichum candidum	7.3
Leptomitus lacteus	3.9
Fusarium aquaeductum	2.3
Algae	
Stigeoclonium tenue	9.3
Ulothrix sp.	3.4
Diatoms	
Navicula spp.	17.9
Fragilaria spp.	11.3
Synedra spp.	11.8
Protozoa	
Ciliates	
Hemiophrys fusidens	28.0
Litonotus fasciola	21.7
Trachelophyllum pusillum	32.9
Chilodonella cucullulus	36.0
Chilodonella uncinata	34.8
Colpidium campylum	22.4
Colpidium colpoda	37.3
Glaucoma scintillans	23.6
Cinetochilum margaritaceum	31.1
Paramecium caudatum	28.0
Paramecium trichium	28.0
Carchesium polypinum	13.0
Vorticella convallaria	13.7
Aspidisca cicada	15.5
Aspidisca lynceus	21.7
Tachysoma pellionella	30.4
Other protozoa	
Colourless micro-flagellates	97.5
Thecate amoebae	3.1
Naked amoebae	1.2

cent of the sites. *Sphaerotilus natans* is one of the sheathed filamentous bacteria and is regarded as the typical 'sewage fungus' organism. Zoogloeal bacteria represents a heterogeneous assemblage of small bacteria all characterised by their ability to extrude a mucilagenous layer enveloping the cells. Taxonomically the group is not well understood and the type organism itself, *Zoogloea ramigera*, is of uncertain status. Incidentally these bacteria are found in several organically polluted environments such as aerobic sewage-treatment processes.

Compared with *Sphaerotilus* and *Zoogloea* all other organisms contributing to sewage fungus occur only infrequently. The most common to occur as dominant organisms are the true fungi *Leptomitus lacteus* and *Geotrichum candidum* which occur in large amounts in 3 and 4 per cent of sites respectively, and the gliding bacterium *Beggiatoa alba* in 5 per cent. *Leptomitus lacteus* is a true fungus and a member of the Phycomycetes. It occurs where there is ample supply of oxygen, calcium and nitrogenous organic matter, so that it most commonly occurs where there is a great dilution by hard water. *Beggiatoa alba* is a sulphur bacterium which forms unbranched filaments of cells in which highly refractile deposits of sulphur can often be seen. This bacterium occurs where both hydrogen sulphide and oxygen are present and oxidises the former to elemental sulphur. It is therefore only found where reduction of sulphate to hydrogen sulphide is taking place near a source of oxygen, which usually means on mud surfaces at the boundary between aerobic and anaerobic environments.

Other filamentous growths include *Flexibacterium* and *Flavobacterium* and, rarely, filamentous algae. Heavy outbreaks of algal growth are most commonly associated with certain types of inorganic pollution, e.g. nitrates, and hence they often form a zone below that of sewage fungus where inorganic pollution may be severe but organic pollution has abated. Indeed, many river algae are known to be intolerant of organic pollution. One species known to be tolerant of both organic and inorganic pollution is *Stigeoclonium tenue* and this is the most frequently found filamentous alga associated with sewage fungus communities. Diatoms are frequently encountered in the slimes but usually in low or moderate numbers, the most common being *Navicula*, *Fragilaria* and *Synedra*.

Most samples of sewage fungus contain protozoa of some description. Surveys show that 97 per cent of the samples contain flagellates and 94 per cent contain ciliates. Colourless micro-flagellates, such as *Bodo caudatus* and many other unidentified species, are the most common flagellated protozoa although a number of species of *Euglena* and its colourless relative *Peranema trichophorum* are also sometimes observed. Both naked amoebae and the testate amoeba *Arcella vulgaris* are occasionally found in small numbers.

A total of 77 ciliated protozoan species have been recorded in sewage fungus and the most commonly seen species are listed in table 3.1. A wider variety of ciliate species is found in sewage fungus communities than in aerobic sewage-treatment processes, perhaps due to the greater diversity of environmental conditions found with the former. However, the ciliate fauna identified is clearly related to that of sewage-treatment processes since nearly 73 per cent of those in polluted waters have been recorded from such processes. If one takes both frequency and abundance data into account then it can be suggested that, other than the attached peritrichous ciliate *Carchesium polypinum*, the most important ciliates are types such as *Colpidium colpoda* and *Chilodonella cucullulus*, which swim or glide between and along the filamentous material. *Carchesium* is found less frequently in the UK than in the USA but it is still the only ciliate likely to be found in sufficient quantities to contribute a substantial amount of filamentous material (stalks) to sewage fungus.

It is evident from above that the sewage fungus curve given in fig 3.1 will overlap with the bacterial and protozoan population curves to a certain extent. Most of the organisms in the protozoan curve have, in fact, already been mentioned. It should be noted that by far the majority of protozoa feed on other organisms, particularly bacteria. Some of the ciliates, such as the two species of *Chilodonella*, are known to feed on filamentous growths. Most of the others feed on suspended bacterial populations. Some ciliates, such as *Litonotus* and *Trachelophyllum*, are carnivorous and prey upon other ciliates.

Interrelations between organisms in sewage fungus

Several statistical methods have been used to obtain insight into the species interrelations of the organisms most frequently found in sewage fungus. When cluster analysis is used, a high degree of association between *Sphaerotilus* and *Zoogloea* is found. Explanations of such associations can be attributed to predator–prey relationships or to species having similar habitat requirements.

The community structure of sewage fungus is shown graphically in fig 3.2. In this diagram branches joining species indicate a relationship and the lengths of the branches between the species indicate the closeness of the relationships. The bacteria and ciliates form an homogeneous group (enclosed within the dotted line) clustered around *Sphaerotilus* and zoogloeal bacteria. This should be interpreted as the main sewage fungus community. However, true fungi and algae all lie outside this group and it has been concluded that they are probably not true sewage fungus components. They are less closely associated with it and more typical of the flora downstream.

Where organic pollution is so severe as to cause total deoxygenation of the water, algae are eliminated. However, where some traces of oxygen remain, the algal population is first depressed but later recovers downstream below the sewage fungus zone. Here the algal population rises significantly above that normally supported in the river water upstream of the pollution source and the species structure changes. In particular *Stigeoclonium tenue* appears to thrive particularly well where there are good

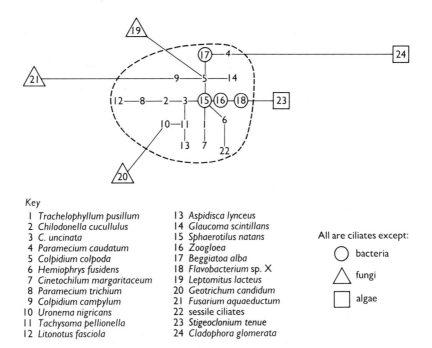

Key

1 *Trachelophyllum pusillum*	13 *Aspidisca lynceus*
2 *Chilodonella cucullulus*	14 *Glaucoma scintillans*
3 *C. uncinata*	15 *Sphaerotilus natans*
4 *Paramecium caudatum*	16 *Zoogloea*
5 *Colpidium colpoda*	17 *Beggiatoa alba*
6 *Hemiophrys fusidens*	18 *Flavobacterium* sp. X
7 *Cinetochilum margaritaceum*	19 *Leptomitus lacteus*
8 *Paramecium trichium*	20 *Geotrichum candidum*
9 *Colpidium campylum*	21 *Fusarium aquaeductum*
10 *Uronema nigricans*	22 sessile ciliates
11 *Tachysoma pellionella*	23 *Stigeoclonium tenue*
12 *Litonotus fasciola*	24 *Cladophora glomerata*

All are ciliates except:

◯ bacteria

△ fungi

▢ algae

Fig 3.2 Minimum spanning tree of common sewage fungus organisms. The tree is drawn to scale, a short distance indicating close association. The dashed line encloses the closest associations which represent the sewage fungus community. From Curtis and Curds, 1971.

supplies of nutrients. Similarly *Cladophora glomerata*, or blanket weed, often forms massive growths and occasionally completely covers the river bed. These growths create particular problems since they tend to deoxygenate the water during the hours of darkness by their respiratory activities.

Specific changes: macro-invertebrates

Until now we have referred only to micro-organisms, but, as fig 3.1 indicates, changes occur in the macro-invertebrate populations as well. Their reactions to organic enrichment are often much clearer than those of the microbes and they are usually easier to identify. Where the water becomes deoxygenated no normal river animals survive, but the larvae of some insects such as the moth-fly *Psychoda* and the rat-tailed maggot *Eristalis* often thrive. Where there is some free oxygen successive populations of bright red tubificid worms, midge larvae (chironomids) and the isopod crustacean *Asellus aquaticus* (the water slater) are often found in extraordinary numbers in beds of blanket weed (*Cladophora*).

Fishes are usually eliminated for long distances from the source of severe organic pollution but reappear in the *Cladophora/Asellus* zone.

Classification of polluted rivers

It is clear from the above description of the effects of organic pollution on the biology of a river that a sequence of events takes place downstream of the organic input as the water undergoes self-purification. Different animals and plants disappear, appear or reappear in various zones. A method of classifying rivers, known as the **saprobic** system, uses these biological zones to indicate the level of pollution present.

It was R. Kolkwitz and M. Marsson, the German hydrobiologists, who pioneered the concept of a saprobic system and developed the early nomenclature for the zones – stretches of water – of polluted rivers and streams receiving sewage and other biodegradable organic wastes. They decided that four successive zones could be defined in a river below the point at which organic waste was discharged according to certain physical and chemical characteristics, as well as by the number and kinds of organisms that inhabited them. Moving from highly polluted to relatively clean water, they called these zones polysaprobic, α-mesosaprobic, β-mesosaprobic and oligosaprobic respectively.

There have been several redefinitions of these zones by other scientists but they are all derived from this early concept. Fig 3.3 compares the most commonly used saprobic systems that have been developed over the years. Traditionally the Kolkwitz and Marsson system has been used by Europeans, whereas the Whipple, Fair and Whipple system is more commonly used in North America.

Kolkwitz and Marsson defined their zones according to the following criteria:

Polysaprobic zone   The zone is characterised chemically by a high concentration of biodegradable organic compounds such as proteins and carbohydrates. There is a decrease in dissolved oxygen concentration and high concentrations of ammonia and hydrogen sulphide are often present. The presence of these compounds in the water gives rise to a high BOD_5. Organisms requiring high levels of dissolved oxygen are absent and fishes avoid the zone. The variety of organisms present in the community is heavily reduced and largely consists of bacteria, the 'sewage fungus' community, tubificid worms and possibly some chironomid larvae.

Mesosaprobic zone   This zone is divided into two sub-zones. The first is the α-mesosaprobic zone which immediately follows the polysaprobic zone. Chemically the water has less organic material present and as a result of earlier decomposition and self-purification has now a preponderance of amino acids rather than proteins. The ammonia concentration has been reduced and nitrates have appeared. Dissolved oxygen is still depressed but

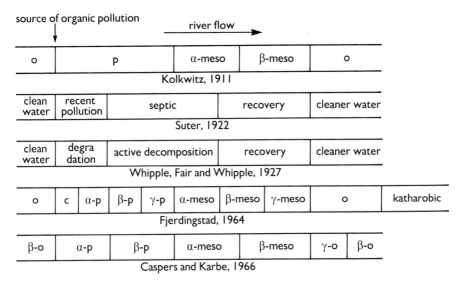

Fig 3.3 A comparison of some major saprobic systems used to classify zones of rivers receiving sewage. o = oligosaprobic, p = polysaprobic, α-meso = α-mesosaprobic, β-meso = β-mesosaprobic, c = coprozoic, α-p = α-polysaprobic, β-p = β-polysaprobic, γ-p = γ-polysaprobic, γ-meso = γ-mesosaprobic, α-o = α-oligosaprobic and β-o = β-oligosaprobic.

there are definite signs of recovery and the BOD_5 has been reduced. The 'sewage fungus' community is still present but declining, as are the other bacterial and protozoan populations. Chironomid larvae may be plentiful and the crustacean *Asellus* may also be present. *Cladophora*, the blanket weed, increases throughout this sub-zone.

In the next sub-zone, the β-mesosaprobic zone, the water quality has further improved. The dissolved oxygen concentration is returning to much higher levels and mineralisation is almost complete. The *Asellus* population is present but declining as is *Cladophora*, the blanket weed. However, a much wider range of animals and plants is present.

Oligosaprobic zone This final zone contains clean water after self-purification has taken place. The dissolved oxygen concentration returns to normal. Organic matter has been degraded and mineralisation completed. The clean-water flora and fauna return with a wide variety of species and there are few bacteria.

Having broadly defined the zones, Kolkwitz and Marsson published long species lists of animals and plants which they found associated with such conditions in polluted rivers and streams in Germany. They classified the organisms as being polysaprobic, α- and β-mesosaprobic and oligosaprobic species and this enabled the level of pollution of a river to be determined by identifying the organisms in it. This led to the concept of biological indices of pollution.

Various other schemes, such as those in fig 3.3, have been introduced but it has to be accepted that no simple, rigid method such as these can hope to take account of the dynamic character of rivers and streams. Many biologists who have studied the pollution of flowing waters have been heavily influenced by such approaches and the ideas of Kolkwitz and Marsson are still frequently expressed in modern research papers. However, their limitations need to be recognised. Probably the biggest flaw in their thinking was the supposition that:

> 'Such a classification presupposes that the respective organisms are uniquely dependent, within relatively narrow limits, on the chemical composition of the water for their distribution and development *in situ*.'
> (Kolkwitz and Marsson, 1909)

In fact very few organisms are uniquely dependent within narrow limits of environmental conditions; indeed it would be foolish to expect such a situation to be common since those with very limited and specialised environmental requirements would be at a great disadvantage when those conditions change, as they inevitably will. Organisms that thrive under a wide range of environmental conditions or are flexible in their requirements are far more likely to succeed when some form of stress is applied.

During the intervening years several European limnologists have introduced classifications which either extend earlier ones or add subdivisions. The Dane Fjerdingstad (1964), for example, added to and subdivided the original four zones into nine by the addition of a coprozoic zone, more highly polluted than the polysaprobic zone, and further subdivision of the poly- and mesosaprobic zones into alpha, beta, and gamma parts. The Czech Sladecek (1969) also extended the saprobic system by including all known waters on his pie diagram on which fig 3.4 is based. He divided the circle into four quadrants which he called katharobic (very clean waters such as ground, spring and drinking waters), limnosaprobic (corresponding to the area of self-purification in an organically polluted river and included within the original saprobic system), eusaprobic (indicating sewage and industrial waste waters undergoing bacterial degradation corresponding to the coprozoic zone of Fjerdingstad). He attributed the fourth quadrant to a trans-saprobic group of waters which included toxins, radioactive substances and inorganic wastes. Including these latter substances into a saprobic system which, from its inception, was only concerned with organic pollution was a mistake and added unnecessary confusion. Thus the fourth quadrant has been omitted from fig 3.4. Sladecek had four zones in the eusaprobic group; these he called ultra-saprobic (a virtually abiotic zone with a BOD_5 of 1000–60 000 mg l^{-1} including industrial wastes such as sugar-beet wastes, etc.), hypersaprobic (containing enormous concentrations of bacteria and fungi, as in some

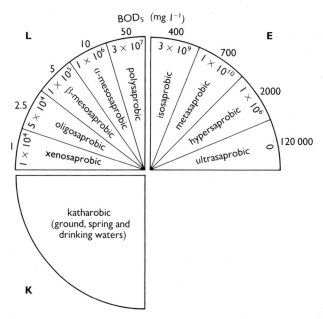

Fig 3.4 Pie diagram illustrating an extension of the saprobic system to include all waters. Three quadrants are shown where K = katharobic, L = limnosaprobic (incorporating the original saprobic system) and E = eusaprobic. Numbers outside and inside the circle refer to upper limits of the BOD_5 and coliform bacteria concentrations respectively. Adapted from Sladecek (1969).

industrial wastes and anaerobic sludges), metasaprobic (containing colourless flagellates as in septic sewage and waters with high sulphur dioxide content) and isosaprobic (containing ciliates and traces of oxygen as in domestic sewage). By including waste waters, Sladecek attempted to include biological waste-treatment processes into the saprobic system apparently discounting the fact that aerobic sewage-treatment processes are quite unlike polluted natural waters in that the dissolved oxygen concentration is kept artificially high even though the concentration of organic matter is equally high. Thus the pie diagram in fig 3.4 has been drawn as a group of unattached quadrants emphasising that there are discontinuities between the three parts.

Protozoa and saprobic systems

The protozoa have always been prominent in saprobic systems and many of the organisms originally listed by Kolkwitz and Marsson belonged to this group. This should be no surprise since many of the organisms which survive or flourish in organically polluted waters are protozoa. The general trend observed in rivers below a source of organic enrichment is an immediate increase in the numbers of bacteria followed by population

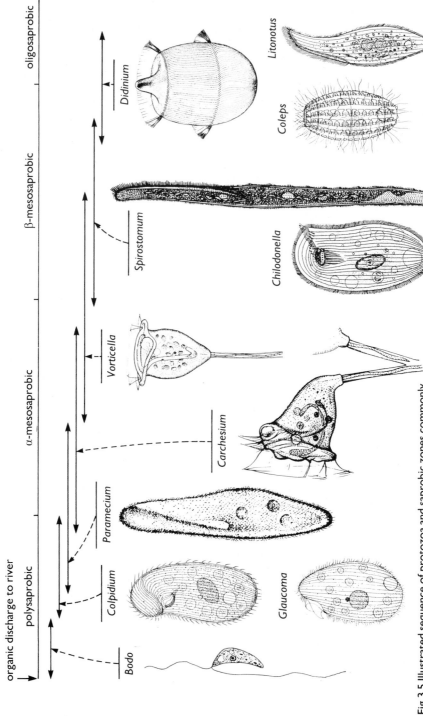

Fig 3.5 Illustrated sequence of protozoa and saprobic zones commonly found in a river receiving sewage.

increases in heterotrophic flagellates such as *Bodo*, and then large numbers of bactivorous ciliates such as *Colpidium*, *Glaucoma*, *Paramecium*, *Cyclidium* and *Carchesium*. This is illustrated in fig 3.5. As conditions improve, other bactivorous ciliates such as *Vorticella* appear, and ciliates such as *Chilodonella* which are able to feed upon filamentous algae and bacteria are followed by omnivorous ciliates such as *Spirostomum* and *Stentor*. Finally, after self-purification is almost complete in the oligosaprobic zone, ciliates appear such as *Coleps* and *Litonotus* which are capable of feeding upon other ciliates. Thus the protozoa follow in a more or less predictable sequence according to their nutritional requirements and the availability of their foodstuffs.

In the protozoa the quantity and type of food available is as important as the saprobic condition of the water. The quantity of food available will determine the potential magnitude of the biomass of protozoa which can be supported, while the type of food will determine the nutritional group of protozoa that survives. Thus in the saprobic system heterotrophic flagellates and bactivorous protozoa are more frequent in the poly- to mesosaprobic zones while carnivorous ciliates are more frequent in the oligosaprobic zones.

The physical and chemical qualities of the water are also important. Some species of bactivorous ciliates occur in heavily polluted waters while others occur more often under lesser polluted conditions. Indeed, in very heavily polluted waters where anaerobic conditions persist for considerable periods, only a few specialised ciliates, such as *Saprodinium* and *Metopus*, which are either strictly anaerobic or **micro-aerophilic** (can grow at very low oxygen concentrations) are able to survive. Many of these anaerobic ciliates have evolved specialised diets, such as sulphur bacteria which are prevalent in such habitats.

Part of the problem of using the protozoa in saprobic systems to predict water quality is that there are few data on their distribution, their precise ranges of environmental preferences and what indicator species actually indicate. This information can be gathered in two ways – directly from observations made in the natural environment or from controlled laboratory experimental work. Most of the original data concerning saprobic systems were gathered from field observations which do not allow controlled effects of specific factors to be evaluated precisely. For example, several protozoologists have turned to using controlled laboratory systems in which a known organic pollutant is added in precise amounts, where the physical and chemical conditions can be continuously monitored and where sampling is simplified. The usual method is to add a known concentration of organic substance to an aquarium which has been seeded with a variety of waters taken from many sources in order to obtain a good inoculum of a wide range of organisms. The biological populations and the physical and chemical characteristics are then monitored against time.

Such studies show that in the first 7–10 days vigorous decomposition takes place by the action mainly of bacteria but also of heterotrophic flagellates. After this time there then follows a stage when distinct successions of ciliate species may be observed. Successive dominant ciliates are usually *Glaucoma scintillans, Cyclidium citrullus, Halteria grandinella, Coleps hirtus, Chilodonella cucullulus, Stylonychia putrina, Paramecium caudatum, Litonotus lamella, Acineta foetida* and *Microthorax* sp. Most of these ciliates are bactivorous but *Coleps, Litonotus* and *Acineta* feed on the other ciliates present. The bactivorous ciliated protozoa are prevalent in the first three weeks when the dissolved oxygen concentration is reduced and ammonia is present. Later, as conditions improve, bactivorous ciliates decline and an autotrophic community consisting of the green flagellates *Euglena* and *Chilomonas* and algal species replace them. Thus the sequence of successive species is regulated by both biological and environmental factors, including the availability of oxygen and food, the presence of the products of decay, by competition and by predator–prey relationships.

Large numbers of experiments like this have been carried out, using different organic substances in different concentrations, and this has allowed scientists to plot the ranges of those environmental parameters under which certain species occur. This has provided some of the basic information concerning the different species which can be used for predictive purposes.

Quantitative saprobic systems

The saprobic systems described so far are qualitative. In order to apply saprobic systems to predict water quality one first has to identify the constituent organisms, list them with the saprobic zone with which they are normally associated and make a qualitative judgement as to the water quality. This means that the method is not only non-quantitative, it is also subjective and depends to a large extent upon the experience and ability of the operator. For these and other reasons various attempts have been made since the mid-1950s to quantify the procedures by introducing mathematical formulae that will reduce the quantity of biological data to a set of numbers or values – the **saprobic index** – that has statistical and scientific meaning.

The first attempts to quantify saprobic systems relied heavily on published lists of animals in previous saprobic systems as sources of primary data. Thus one early method used data derived from the Kolkwitz and Marsson system. For each of the saprobic zones the abundance of each species was measured on a linear basis of 1–7 where 1 represents a single sighting and 7 indicates that the organism is abundant. This method calculated the saprobic index (S) of the water on a percentage basis from the equation:

$$S = \frac{\Sigma(\mathrm{o} + \beta)}{\Sigma(\mathrm{o} + \beta + \alpha + \mathrm{p})} \times 100$$

Table 3.2. *Theoretical saprobic valencies and indicator values of the five species A–E. Here an additional non-polluted or xenosaprobic zone (x) has been included*

| Species | Saprobic valencies (SV) for each saprobic zone (total of 10 points) | | | | | Indicator value (1–5) |
	x	o	β	α	p	g
A	3	3	3	1		1
B	5	5				3
C	4	6				3
D	2	7	1			3
E		8	2			4

where o = oligo, β = β-meso, α = α-meso and p = polysaprobic classes. That is, the sums of the semi-quantitative estimates of animals found which represent the better quality saprobic zones are divided by the sums of those which represent all saprobic classes. Thus if a high proportion of organisms associated with low levels of pollution is present the saprobic index tends towards a low value.

Such early methods did not take into account the fact that many species may be found within a range of saprobic zones, not just one. To overcome this deficiency Zelinka and Marvan (1961) developed a method in which a total of 10 points were distributed to each species. The points, or saprobic valencies, were distributed according to how commonly the species was found to be associated with each of the saprobic zones. Thus in table 3.2, which lists the saprobic valencies of five species A–E, it will be seen that although the sum of saprobic valencies always totals ten points, the valencies are distributed differently and unevenly between the saprobic zones. Additionally the saprobic valencies were weighted by use of the indicator value, g, which varies from 1 to 5 according to the tolerance of the species and its ability to survive in the various zones. Thus a high value for g shows that the organism has a very limited distribution range and is therefore an excellent indicator organism whereas a low value for g shows that the organism is very tolerant and may be found over a wide range of organically polluted conditions.

Notice that species A which may be found in a wide range of zones has a low indicator value whereas the intolerant species E which is almost always found in the oligosaprobic zone has a high value.

Next the actual numbers (h) of each species found must be counted. The calculation then proceeds as illustrated in table 3.3. The numbers (h) are multiplied first by the indicator value (g) and the result (hg) is then multiplied by the saprobic valencies (SV) taken from table 3.2 for each zone. Totals for all species in each saprobic zone are obtained by simple addition and the averages obtained by dividing the totals by the sum of the hg in the fourth column.

It is these averages that are used to estimate the saprobic index of the site

Table 3.3. *Calculation of the saprobity of a theoretical site using the five indicator species A–E*

Species	Abundance	Indicator value		hg SV				
	h	g	hg	x	o	β	α	p
A	69	1	69	207	207	207	69	—
B	31	3	93	465	465	—	—	—
C	30	3	90	360	540	—	—	—
D	42	3	126	252	882	126	—	—
E	8	4	32	—	256	64	—	—
Totals			410	1284	2350	397	69	0
Averages				3.13	5.73	0.97	0.17	0

from which the animals were collected. Clearly in table 3.3 the average of 5.73 calculated for the oligosaprobic zone is much higher than the average for any other zone. Thus the site would be termed oligosaprobic. While this method is more time consuming than qualitative methods, it has the potential of being more accurate since it is based upon precise calculations of the frequency of the species rather than rough estimates.

Limitations of the use of saprobic systems

Although saprobic systems have been widely used by hydrobiologists in continental Europe they have been met with criticism from scientists in the UK and USA. Five major objections are raised:

1   The necessity to identify the organisms to the species level requires considerable amounts of time from highly trained personnel.
2   Our scant knowledge of the ecological characteristics and requirements of the individual organisms and their communities is incomplete.
3   There are considerable difficulties in obtaining a statistically sound representative sample from aquatic habitats.
4   There is a failure to recognise that each pollutant and stream has an element of uniqueness about it. A saprobic system makes generalised statements and assumptions that are not necessarily valid.
5   The saprobic system is, or should be, restricted to pollution caused by domestic sewage or similar organic wastes. It should not be used for the many other types of pollutants such as inorganic, toxic and industrial wastes.

Saprobic systems can only be properly applied to organic wastes, such as domestic sewage for which it was devised. Other pollutants have different effects. For example, organic pollution results in a reduction in the number of species present but an increase in the numbers of individuals of some of the species left. This was demonstrated many years ago by Ruth Patrick, the American ecologist, who pioneered the use of diatoms as indicator organisms. She compared the diversity of polluted and non-polluted sites

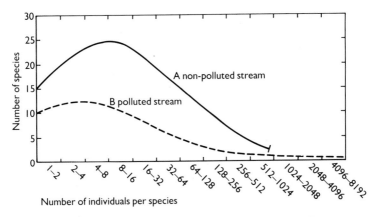

Fig 3.6 A graphic comparison of diatom communities from two different environments. After Patrick (1954).

by plotting the number of species found against the numbers of specimens in each of the species (fig 3.6). Communities followed log–normal distributions which changed their shape according to the amount of pollution applied. In a non-polluted stream the distribution curve shape is tall and narrow indicating that the number of species is high but most occur in small numbers. Distribution in a polluted stream is low but wide indicating the presence of fewer species, some in large numbers. However, when the pollutant is toxic the community change is different since numbers of both species and individuals are depressed.

For many years the aim of many ecologists has been the invention of a method of describing the level of pollution which does not depend upon the type of pollutant. To date the most promising approach has been centred around the mathematical description of community diversity in the form of an index. The methods proposed are all based upon the concept that the structure of normal communities of organisms may be changed by perturbations in the environment and the degree of change from the norm may be used to assess the strength or intensity of the environmental stress. No assumptions are made about the type of stress involved and the methods can therefore be applied to any form of pollution. Unfortunately there is, as yet, no general agreement about what the mathematical description between the number of species and abundance of individuals should be.

However, in spite of the criticisms, it should also be understood that analysis of biological systems has an advantage over chemical analysis. The latter only supplies specific pieces of information whereas analyses of communities of organisms gives integrated overall data that cannot be obtained by chemical means. The use of saprobic systems has value as long as it is applied and interpreted in an intelligent and flexible manner.

Other biological indicators of pollution

We have concentrated on saprobic systems because we are predominantly concerned with protozoa, but it should be realised that there are many other methods available which aim to use animals and plants as indicators of pollution. These utilise benthic, macro-invertebrate animals as the major indicator organisms. Samples are taken in various ways, by net and hand, to obtain a representative sample and the river is then scored according to the presence or absence of certain key groups to determine what is termed the biotic index. Some of the fauna need only be identified to genus or family level while others need specific determination. As most of the macro-invertebrates are easier to identify than protists it is perhaps not surprising that these methods are more commonly used in more countries than the saprobic system.

4

Potable water supplies

Sources and contamination of water supplies

In nature, water circulates through the **hydrological cycle**. Water vapour from the sea rises to form clouds which condense as rain. Once on land, rainwater flows back towards the sea in rivers or underground as groundwater. It then evaporates to complete the cycle.

Water can become contaminated virtually anywhere in the hydrological cycle. In the process of condensation and precipitation the water dissolves gases from the air and entrains dust particles. Carbon dioxide from the atmosphere reacts with water to form a weak acid which aids in the dissolution of the airborne dust particles so that by the time the rain meets the ground it can already contain up to 10 mg 1^{-1} of dissolved and suspended solids, although it is rare for such a concentration to be reached under normal circumstances. As the water flows in rivers, or seeps through the soil and travels underground as groundwater, it comes into contact with a wide variety of dissolved and suspended organic and inorganic materials. The dissolved organic substances may be suitable for the growth of micro-organisms and so water can also become microbiologically contaminated.

Natural waters are highly diverse in character but can be categorised simply according to their origins and a range of properties such as colour, turbidity (caused by a wide range of suspended solids including bacteria), taste, odour, hardness, pH, etc.

In upland areas where the bedrock is composed of materials such as granite which do not readily dissolve, the streams are often clear and sparkling in appearance. This upland water is usually soft, that is to say it contains only low concentrations of the calcium and magnesium salts which react with soap to cause a scum. Soft waters such as these often have a low

41

pH and may be corrosive. In some upland limestone areas the water may be moderately hard with a higher pH, and those which flow through peat may become coloured because of the presence of humic and fulvic acids. Lowland waters can also be hard or soft but in general contain more suspended materials and higher concentrations of dissolved solids.

Groundwaters are often very clear with very low bacterial concentrations, indeed until about 20 years ago they were considered to be pristine and virtually sterile. Pollution of groundwaters has changed that view and even non-polluted groundwater is recognised to contain a bacterial flora, albeit in low numbers. Certain groundwaters, such as spa waters, contain very high concentrations of dissolved salts and those in chalk areas are usually very hard.

Treating contamination

Several different methods, or more commonly combinations of methods, to deal with contaminants are available. The actual methods chosen will depend mainly on the source of the raw water and its constituent impurities. For example, some groundwaters may be sufficiently pure as to only require some form of disinfection before use whilst polluted river water will require a combination of several physical, chemical and biological processes before it is ready for human consumption. In dealing with contamination the water industry has to continually change its methods in response to changing demands. For example, in the UK, large activated carbon filters are now being installed to remove pesticides and other impurities in response to new standards being imposed. Waters used for some industrial purposes may not need a rigorous range of purifying processes. Other industries, on the other hand, may require a greater proportion of dissolved inorganic minerals to be removed before use. Thus it is not possible within the scope of this book to present a complete picture of all treatment methods. Only the most commonly used systems are described. They normally include one or more of the processes of storage, coagulation and clarification, roughing filtration, slow sand filtration and disinfection (fig 4.1).

Storage and preliminary treatment

Water stored in reservoirs undergoes a series of changes in its physical, chemical and biological character which can be either beneficial or detrimental to the objective of producing water fit for human consumption. The major benefits that simple storage in a reservoir imparts are the reduction in suspended solids and bacterial concentrations. The quiescent conditions in a reservoir allow much of the suspended particulate matter to settle out. However, while this is beneficial, it enables light to penetrate further into the reservoir water and this tends to increase the algal population present. The development of algal populations is undesirable

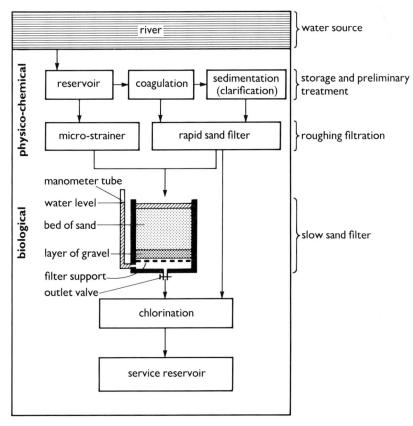

Fig 4.1 Diagrammatic outline of the processes used to produce potable water including a section through a slow sand filter.

since their presence can block filters quickly and sometimes cause taste problems.

During the summer, stored water may become thermally stratified as in some natural lakes. A warm, less dense, upper water layer or **epilimnion** covers the lower, more dense, layer or **hypolimnion**. They are separated by a narrow discontinuity layer, the **thermocline**, in which the temperature and therefore density changes rapidly. The thermocline suppresses downward transport of dissolved substances such as oxygen and this can result in the hypolimnion becoming anoxic if the oxygen demand of water and mud is greater than the oxygen input across the thermocline. In situations where the epilimnion contains a large population of algae and the hypolimnion is deoxygenated it is difficult to find an appropriate depth from which to extract water. To overcome this the thermocline must be prevented or destroyed by physical methods involving a gentle mixing procedure such as the introduction of air bubbles at the appropriate depth.

De-stratification of a storage reservoir by such methods can significantly change the biological character of the stored water. In light, algae fix dissolved carbon dioxide to form new organic compounds. When there is a lot of light available these organic materials are converted into the growth of new tissue and the population increases. In low light levels this does not occur. The relative effect of light on an algal population will depend on the ratio of the depth through which the algae are mixed and the depth to which the light can penetrate. The greater the mixed depth relative to the light penetration depth, the less able are the algae to grow. Thus when the mixed depth is increased by de-stratification there is every chance of a significant reduction in the algal population followed by changes in the whole biota.

Whilst the treatment function of storage reservoirs is important, it is nearly always of secondary importance to their main purpose which is to provide a reliable supply of water. In some small reservoirs, where the storage time is only a matter of seven days or so, their major role is to smooth out daily variations in water quality, although they may be closed to provide a short-term reserve in the event of river pollution. The larger reservoirs are of two types – **impounding reservoirs** which are usually formed by building a dam across a valley, and **pumped-storage reservoirs** which are often built on flat land by constructing earthen embankments. Impounding reservoirs receive a significant amount of water direct from rainfall over a wide area and the water is variable and beyond control. In pumped-storage reservoirs there is more opportunity to select water from the river when conditions are favourable.

In the UK an aeration stage is sometimes interposed between storage and treatment. This has the advantage of reducing the amounts of undesirable gases, such as carbon dioxide and hydrogen sulphide, dissolved in the water and increasing the level of dissolved oxygen, all of which improves the final taste.

Coagulation and clarification

In water where there is a high level of suspended solids present, sometimes as much as tens of thousands mg l^{-1}, or where there is an obvious colour, a clarification stage may be essential to achieve an appropriate water turbidity standard.

All clarification processes depend upon the addition of a coagulating chemical to destabilise or precipitate the colloidal or soluble impurities present. The aim is to produce a floc that will either settle or float so that it can be easily removed as a sludge from the water. Aluminium or iron salts are the most usual coagulants used because of their cost effectiveness. Probably the most widely used are aluminium sulphate ('alum') and ironIII sulphate (ferric sulphate), normally in concentration ranges 10–75 mg l^{-1}, although ironIII chloride (ferric chloride) may be used in other countries. There is now general public concern over the use of aluminium as a coagulant since there is a possible relationship between aluminium intake and Altzheimer's disease. This has led at least one water authority to revert to using iron sulphate again. These coagulants react only within specific and narrow pH ranges and are most effective at a particular pH, so either lime or liquid caustic soda or sulphuric acid are added to achieve the optimum pH.

In recent years water treatment has undergone a revolution with the introduction of poly-electrolyte coagulants (heavy long-chain synthetic polymers) and coagulant aids. These new chemicals have enabled clarifiers to be operated at much higher rates and at the same time produce a better quality water. They are more expensive but the dose levels are often extremely low and become cost effective when one considers that the size, and hence the cost, of clarification plants can be considerably reduced.

Following the addition of coagulants the precipitates must be allowed to flocculate into visible particles if they are to be removed from the water body. Flocculation is usually accomplished by means of slow stirring followed by a quiescent period for sedimentation. In most modern clarifiers some of the sludge is recirculated and mixed with raw incoming water in order to accelerate the capture of the microfloc particles produced by coagulation. Other clarifiers ensure that a blanket of floc particles is maintained on a rising flow of water so that the microflocs are 'filtered out' as they pass through the blanket. Yet others remove the sludge by microbubbles generated from super-saturated water which float it upwards to the surface.

Roughing filtration

Roughing filtration is commonly used as a non-chemical way to remove some suspended matter and enhance the chemical quality of the water before slow sand filtration. The most common methods of roughing filtration are either **microstraining** or **rapid gravity filtration**. Microstrainers remove suspended particulate matter by straining through a fine metallic fabric filter mounted on a rotating drum. Only particulate matter is removed and there is no reduction in colour, colloidal turbidity or ammonia concentration. However, rapid gravity filtration involves the filtration of the water through open rapid sand filters at a high rate (6–8 m h^{-1}). Some reduction in bacterial concentration and other suspended solids are accomplished as well as some improvement in colour and oxidation, and almost complete removal of normal levels of ammonia. It is apparent from these results that while most of the action is physical some biological processes are also proceeding.

Slow sand filtration

There are two methods of **sand filtration** in use today, **slow** and **rapid**. Both rely on physical and physico-chemical modes of action but slow sand filters have the addition of a major biological component. Slow sand filtration has been in use in Britain since early in the nineteenth century and although there has been a relative decline in its use, a very large volume of water continues to be successfully purified by this method. Approximately 30 per cent of all surface water in Britain is still treated by slow sand filtration in conjunction with the other processes mentioned above.

Rapid filters which do not rely on biological processes are cheaper to install and operate than slow sand filters, and are not affected by the colder winter temperatures of, for example, North America. However, the major advantages of slow sand filters are that they are simple and reliable to operate, and are safe and stable in their output quality. In 1970, the World Health Organisation took a fresh look at slow sand filtration and is now encouraging its use in some developing countries and rural areas.

Fig 4.1 illustrates a section through a slow sand filter. The principal filtration agent is a bed of sand and when a clean bed is first established it is filled with raw water which is allowed to leave very slowly. Over the next few days, as the quality of the filtrate improves, the outlet valve is opened to the optimum flow rate (50–300 mm h^{-1}). Once the valve is fully open no other action is necessary until a loss of water head, as indicated on a manometer, shows that the filter is becoming clogged. At the Thames Valley (UK) treatment works, for example, a filter can be expected to run for about 60 days before drainage and cleaning are necessary. Cleaning involves the rolling aside of a mat of filamentous algae which may take up a volume of 70 m^3 ha^{-1} (a wet weight of several tonnes) and the subsequent removal of the surface layers (1–2 cm) of sand either manually, mechanically or hydraulically.

The efficacy of slow sand filtration has been well documented and, generally, the process removes better than 90 per cent of the bacterial concentration applied. While the physical mechanisms involved in the removal of suspended particulate matter by sand filtration have been understood for a long time it is only in the last 20 years that some of the biological processes responsible for bacterial removal have been investigated. There is an obvious, complex microbiological community, the 'smutdecke', at the sand–water interface but, with the exception of the algae, its components remained undescribed until relatively recently. The microbial community and the role of the protozoa in this process will be discussed in chapter 6.

Disinfection

Disinfection, usually by adding chlorine to a residual concentration of 0.2–0.7 mg l^{-1}, is an essential stage of water treatment and if properly applied ensures the complete destruction of all harmful pathogenic bacteria and viruses. It prevents the spread of waterborne diseases such as typhoid, paratyphoid, cholera, dysentery, gastroenteritis and leptospiral jaundice. However, certain waterborne protozoan diseases may

Table 4.1. *Some examples of WHO guidelines for drinking water quality. From Guidelines to Drinking Water Quality, WHO, Geneva, 1982*

Characteristic	Action level
Arsenic	0.05 mg l^{-1}
Aluminium	0.2
Lead	0.05
Mercury	0.001
Nitrite nitrogen	1.0
Chloride	250
Sulphate	400
Hardness as $CaCO_3$	500
Total dissolved solids	1000
DDT	1.0 μg l^{-1}
Lindane	3.0
pH	6.5–8.5
Coliform bacteria	absent in 100 ml

require higher concentrations of chlorine to be really effective and this will be discussed in chapter 8. Chlorine is almost the universal choice of disinfectant because it is effective against a wide range of micro-organisms, simple to apply and relatively cheap. However, there is growing evidence which strongly suggests that chlorination can produce traces of potentially carcinogenic chlor-organic by-products when applied to waters containing industrial pollutants or even natural organic material. These findings have resulted in the search for other disinfecting agents and attention has been mainly focused on the use of chlorine dioxide and ozone.

Drinking water quality standards

In the UK, water authorities supplying water for human consumption are under a statutory obligation to supply a pure and wholesome water. Taylor (1958) defined a water as pure and wholesome if:

'It is free from visible suspended matter, colour, odour and taste, from all objectionable bacteria indicative of the presence of disease-producing organisms, and contains no dissolved matter of mineral or organic origin which in quality or quantity would render it dangerous to health, and will not dissolve substances injurious to health.'

While this is a good qualitative description it does not define maximum allowable concentrations of contaminants which are necessary when introducing quality control standards. Many countries have opted to set mandatory standards for the quality of both raw and potable waters, frequently using the International Standards for Drinking Water proposed by the World Health Organisation (table 4.1). However, others such as Canada and the USA have adopted standards unique to themselves though broadly similar to those laid down by the WHO.

Britain and some other countries did not originally adopt the mandatory standards approach on the grounds that no rigid water standards can be set to take account of the many local factors which affect the suitability of given types of water for their intended uses. Further it was argued that rigidly imposed raw water standards do not give our normally highly competent water managers sufficient leeway to make use of their expertise and experience. While both approaches have advantages and disadvantages the current involvement of the EC now means that the quality of drinking water in the UK is effectively controlled by the standards described in the European Community Directive relating to the quality of water intended for human consumption. Water that does not meet the EC Directive standards is not 'wholesome', while water that meets them is usually so but in some cases may not be depending on guidance given by the Department of the Environment. The EC has threatened legal action against certain countries, including the UK, for producing some localised water supplies that are not 'wholesome'. However, in spite of this, it should not be forgotten that unlike most other European countries, most of the population in Britain have received piped supplies of good quality drinking water for about a century and quite elaborate methods are used to achieve this from raw water supplies which may be polluted.

5

Sewage-treatment processes

Over the past 150 years various processes have been developed to reduce the amount of organic pollution reaching natural fresh and marine waters. These processes began with land treatment in which sewage was sprayed directly on to areas of land where microbial action degraded the organic complexes as the waste waters trickled through the soil. However, these 'sewage farms' are not sufficiently efficient to deal with the ever-increasing quantities of domestic and industrial waste waters that are produced by the modern world and the production of high-quality effluents is now a series of highly technological processes.

Fig 5.1 shows the layout of the processes used in a typical large sewage-treatment works in the UK, designed to produce a high-quality effluent before discharge into a river used as a source for public water supply. Such an effluent would typically need to satisfy a 10:10:10 standard, indicating that the suspended solids, BOD_5 and ammoniacal nitrogen concentrations did not exceed 10 mg 1^{-1}. The processes are normally divided into three major categories commonly referred to as **primary**, **secondary** and **tertiary treatment**. All methods of primary treatment are purely physical, all secondary treatments are biological and tertiary treatments can be either. Sewage-treatment works situated on inland sites in the UK use primary and secondary treatment processes as a minimum and probably some form of 'polishing' or tertiary treatment. However, those works located around the coasts may only use some primary-treatment processes before disposal in the sea. This is not the case in the USA where government legislation in the 1970s made it necessary for all communities to use both primary and secondary treatment processes before effluent disposal to land and coastal waters. This may soon apply in Europe. Debate is taking place in the European Parliament to introduce

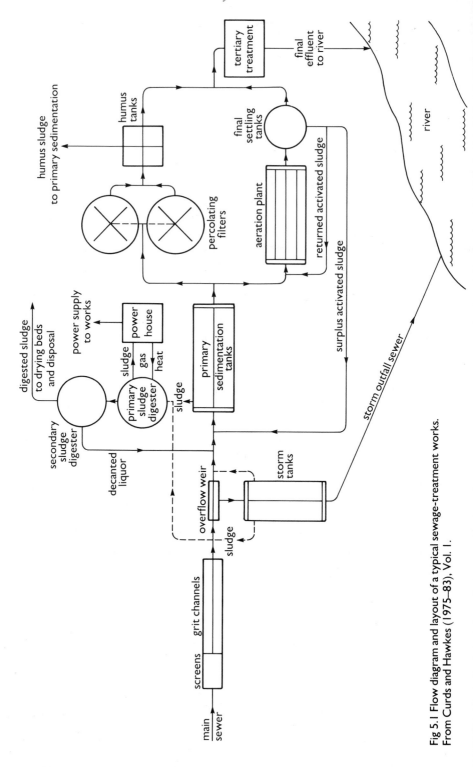

Fig 5.1 Flow diagram and layout of a typical sewage-treatment works. From Curds and Hawkes (1975–83), Vol. I.

legislation to prevent the disposal of sewage into coastal waters by European countries.

In the following account each type of treatment is described. In each secondary and tertiary treatment process the basic biology is outlined but details of the role of protozoa are left to chapter 6.

Primary treatment

Most domestic sewage in the UK receives some form of primary treatment to remove gross solids. Certainly all sewage treated at inland sites receives primary treatment and commonly works situated on coastal sites use some form of primary treatment. Usually, the first operation involves the removal of coarse solids such as rags, paper, sticks and other rubbish by screening. Typically screens are constructed from a number of parallel metal bars regularly spaced a few inches apart. In modern works these screens are cleaned by mechanical raking, the operation being controlled automatically to correspond with changes in sewage flow by means of either a fixed time schedule or changes in the differential hydrostatic head across the screens. This is probably the most unpleasant operation encountered in a sewage-treatment works and in many the screens have been replaced by mechanical shredding devices known as comminutors. Grit collected by the flow of sewage on its way to the treatment works is removed and washed at some early stage, either just before or after screening, by sedimentation, allowing the denser grit particles to be removed but not the lighter organic solids. Usually this operation is carried out in grit channels but other methods are also used. At the end of these purely physical processes the sewage is ready for further treatment, although, as has been said, in the case of coastal sites it is still only too frequently pumped out to sea, a practice that will cease in the near future (see previous page). Usually between two-thirds and three-quarters of the remaining suspended solids following preliminary treatment can be removed by further sedimentation under gravity within a period of a few hours. The sludge which collects at the base of such sedimentation tanks is removed by mechanical scrapers and is treated biologically in anaerobic digesters which are described later (see page 65). The supernatant sewage which flows out from primary sedimentation tanks is called settled sewage and is ready for some form of secondary treatment.

Secondary treatment

All forms of secondary treatment are biological and rely on the growth of micro-organisms to remove dissolved and suspended materials or to convert them into more acceptable compounds. These processes are aerobic and all involve some means of introducing atmospheric oxygen into the sewage and associated microbial populations. Many methods have been devised over the years but the two most commonly used methods are

biological filters (also called **percolating filters** and **trickling filters**) and the **activated-sludge process**. The two processes are equally used for domestic sewage in the UK. Biological filters are more common in rural districts and activated sludge more common in the larger towns and cities.

Of the conventional biological processes used in secondary treatment, activated sludge is the most intensive and therefore requires least land. This is the prime reason why it is more common in urban areas where land is at a premium. However, activated sludge requires more energy because of the need to pump air and liquids continuously. Also it is more susceptible to changes in external conditions such as toxic discharges or sudden changes in sewage strength. Although activated sludge is more manageable it demands greater operational skills. Thus the choice of system depends largely upon its location, sometimes on the type of effluent to be treated and on the availability of skilled operators. Both processes are equally capable of producing high-quality effluents.

Biological or percolating filters

Of the various methods which have been devised to rapidly purify sewage by aerobic microbial oxidation, biological filtration has proved to be one of the most successful. It is the longest established secondary treatment process still in widespread use and most readers will at least already be familiar with its appearance. Filters are a common sight to travellers as many sewage works are situated close to railway lines.

Typically there is a circular bed of mineral aggregate (clinker or stones) over which a slowly rotating distributor arm discharges settled sewage. The name 'filter' is misleading, stemming from the early days of the development of the process when it was assumed that the purification processes were brought about by physical filtration. Although trapping of some suspended solids is undoubtedly a part of the purification processes, the percolating filter is essentially a biological reactor. The biomass is a film on the surfaces of the filter medium which is packed within the retaining wall. The use of the term 'bacteria bed' is a slightly better description than 'filter' but since the microbial populations represented include not only bacteria but also protozoa, algae and fungi, as well as a whole host of macro-invertebrate populations, perhaps the term 'biological bed' would be even more appropriate. However, the term biological filter is normally used along with percolating filter and trickling filter, terms used commonly in the UK and USA respectively.

The biological filter had its origin in the early sewage farm methods of land treatment where sewage was allowed to percolate through under-drained areas of porous soil. Periods of several hours between successive applications of sewage allowed air to penetrate the soil and keep the process aerobic. However, such methods require enormous areas of land. For example, at the turn of the century the City of Birmingham was using some 2800 acres of land for the purpose and, more significantly, adding

1½ acres per week in an attempt to keep abreast of the growing population. Around 1889, investigations were started in the USA at the Lawrence Experimental Station of the Massachusetts State Board of Health to ascertain the effectiveness of various local sands, soils, gravels and natural aggregates to treat sewage. In some experiments it was found that sewage treatment was more effective using the coarser gravels and aggregates than with the finer sands; it took place at higher rates and the coarse materials did not clog so easily. From observations such as these it was realised that purification did not depend upon physical filtration but on biochemical oxidation processes brought about during the 'slow movement of the sewage in a thin film over the surfaces of stones covered with biological slimes, in the presence of air' (Clark, 1930).

There is no doubt that the basic principles of the modern biological filter were established in the USA at the Lawrence Experimental Station. However, the initial practical implementation of these findings was carried out in the UK where the need for intensive treatment was most urgent. The first large-scale percolating filter installation, extending over some 10 acres, was installed in Salford in 1892 whereas the first municipal trickling filter in the USA was installed in Atlanta, Georgia in 1903. By 1908, percolating filters were in use all over the UK and eastern parts of the USA, and the subsequent use of travelling distributors rather than static systems improved the uniformity of application of the liquid.

The biological filter serves essentially to provide an extensive area of aerated surfaces over which the waste water undergoing treatment can flow freely and uniformly. The microbial populations colonise the surfaces and form a static biological film. The structure of a typical filter is shown in fig 5.2. It consists of a foundation floor supporting the filter medium and serving to collect effluent draining from the bed, a 2-metre deep bed of medium consisting of a graded mineral aggregate such as clinker or stones retained by an encircling wall; and a distributor system for applying the waste waters in a uniform manner to the surface of the filter medium. These are basic features upon which there has been wide scope for development and variation. By the mid-1950s media fabricated from lightweight high-strength materials became commercially available and since then a wide range of types and patterns have been marketed. The lighter-weight plastics reduce the need for thick and costly retaining walls and by improving the proportion and distribution of the geometry of the internal spaces or voids, efficiency was increased. However, the cost of plastic media is considerably greater than that of aggregate materials and thus plastic is still used to a lesser extent. The greatest impact of plastic media was that it gave the treatment-plant designer increased scope by which, for example, to develop processes for special purposes that would not have been possible using conventional aggregate media.

Basic biology   When a new filter is brought into operation, although there is some immediate reduction in the BOD_5 of the waste water, the removal

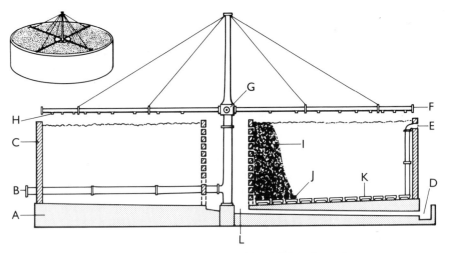

Fig 5.2 Section through a typical biological filter. A foundation floor,
B feed pipe, C retaining wall, D effluent channel, E ventilation pipe,
F distributor arm, G rotary seal, H jets, I main bed of medium, J base layer
of medium, K filter tiles, L central well for effluent collection. From Curds
and Hawkes (1975–83), Vol. 2.

efficiency is very poor in comparison to an established filter. A filter needs
to mature through the establishment of populations of a wide range of
microbial and animal life. Maturation takes a period of several weeks while
the microbial populations become established but it is months before all the
macro-invertebrate animals have colonised the filter. Initially it is the
bacterial and fungal populations that begin to grow on those surfaces
wetted by the sewage. As they grow they use up the organic and inorganic
constituents of the sewage, and, as time goes on, they grow into areas that
do not directly receive a flow of sewage. This is important since it greatly
increases the surface area of the biological film responsible for the
purification processes. In due course, this film becomes a close and
complex association of bacteria, fungi, protozoa, and macro-invertebrates –
mainly flies and worms. Some algae occur in the top-most layers exposed to
light.

Under normal circumstances bacteria form the bulk of the active biomass
of the biological film. In filters treating domestic sewage, bacteria forming
finger-like growths (zoogloeal growths), composed of a jelly-like matrix
into which the bacteria are embedded, form the basic structure of the film.
Early workers referred to the bacterium *Zoogloea ramigera* as being probably the most characteristic organism in the upper layers of a filter.
However, recent studies show that many bacteria have the ability to grow in
colonies of this appearance and it is now known that several Gram-negative
rod bacteria inhabit biological filters. These bacterial populations are not
like those of the inflowing sewage which originate mainly in human faeces.
They are more related to those found in flowing natural waters, including

genera such as *Achromobacter, Alcaligenes, Flavobacterium, Pseudomonas* and *Zoogloea*. Nitrifying bacteria such as *Nitrosomonas* and *Nitrobacter* may be found in the lower regions of filters treating domestic sewage which contain ammoniacal compounds.

Fungi can be a major component of the biological film, particularly in the upper levels of filters, but when this is the case certain problems arise. Heavy growths of fungal mycelium tend to block the pathways through which the sewage percolates and pools of liquid occur on the filter surface – a phenomenon known as 'ponding'. Blockage of the flow pathways reduces flow and inhibits aeration of the filter so promoting anaerobic zones. Furthermore, heavy fungal growths may support very large populations of fly larvae and result in the emergence of sufficient flies to create a nuisance in the kitchens of neighbouring households. Six fungi commonly account for the bulk of the mycelium content of the film: *Sepedonium* sp., *Subbaromyces splendens, Ascoidea rubescens, Fusarium aquaeductuum, Geotrichum candidum* and *Trichosporon cutaneum*. They are most abundant in the top 15 cm layer. Besides flourishing on dissolved organic material, some fungi in treatment plants live saprophytically on dead insects, and others as predators of protozoa, nematodes and rotifers. However, their role in the ecosystem and purification processes is probably a minor one.

As the waste water flows over the biological film the colloidal and fine solids flocculate and deposit on to the film's surface where they are degraded by extracellular enzymes produced by both bacteria and fungi. Some of the solids are consumed directly by macro-invertebrates and suspended bacteria by protozoa and possibly rotifers.

As a result of microbial growth and the flocculation of suspended solids the film in the filter tends to accumulate. Only a thin microbial slime is required for efficient purification and if the film becomes too thick the inner regions tend to become anaerobic. The thickness of the biological film results from a large number of interacting factors. Those mentioned above tend to increase the film thickness but others, such as endogenous metabolism, tend to reduce it. The onset of anaerobic conditions may cause the death and autolysis of the microbial populations deep within the film which disintegrate and are washed out of the filter. There are also non-microbial factors to be taken into account. Enchytraeid worms, lumbricid worms, collembola and dipteran (fly) larvae all feed voraciously on the solids, converting them into humus which is flushed from the system.

The macro-invertebrate populations found commonly in biological filters include annelid worms such as *Aelosoma hemprichi, Enchytraeus* spp., *Lumbricillus lineatus, Nais elinguis, Nais variabilis, Eisenia foetida* and *Eiseniella tetraedra* as well as a variety of insects including collembola, coleoptera and hymenoptera but principally diptera such as *Psychoda* spp., *Hydrobaenus* spp. and *Leptocera* spp. The annelids, collembola and the majority of fly larvae feed on the film, and there is clear evidence that, under normal operational procedures practised in the UK, their activities are extremely important in preventing the filters being blocked. They are most effective during the summer when increased temperatures promote greater biological activity, since, although the rate of film growth is about twice that recorded during the winter, ponding rarely occurs in summer. Experiments with small replicate laboratory filters operated with and without the different major components of macro-invertebrates have demonstrated that without the invertebrates the filters quickly become clogged and produce inferior effluents.

By feeding on the film, insects and annelids perform three functions. Firstly, they convert some of the film to carbon dioxide and other simple substances which are excreted. It has been estimated that macro-invertebrate respiration accounts for between 2 and 10 per cent of the total organic carbon oxidised in a filter. Secondly, they change the character of the film by converting much of it into faecal pellets which may aid bacterial degradation. Thirdly, they convert the film into animal biomass which in the case of diptera leave the filter as 'flying biomass'. These three activities all serve to reduce the quantity of biological film within the filter and enable more sewage to be treated than would otherwise be possible.

Activated-sludge process

Although early experiments in Britain and America had demonstrated the possibility of treating sewage by aeration, the period required to obtain a high degree of purification was so long as to make the idea uneconomic. In these experiments the solids or sludge produced during successive oxidations were discarded. However, the classic experiments of E. Arden and W.T. Lockett (1914a and b) in Manchester on the 'oxidation of sewage without the aid of filters', showed that the aeration period could be reduced from about five weeks to less than 24 hours if the sludge solids were retained. These solids were, 'for reference purposes and failing a better term', called 'activated sludge'. In further experiments, it was found that the aeration period could be reduced to about six hours and an effluent 'quite equal to that yielded by an efficient bacterial filter' was achieved provided a sufficient concentration (about 3000 mg 1^{-1}) of sludge was used and that there was adequate mixing and aeration. From these early laboratory experiments there quickly developed the first continuous-flow activated-sludge plant which opened in April 1916 at Worcester sewage-treatment works. Since then the process has become established throughout the world as an accepted method for the secondary treatment of sewage and many industrial organic effluents.

An outline of the most common type of activated-sludge process is given in fig 5.3. Settled sewage enters a tank where it is aerated with activated sludge for a period of between 3 and 8 hours. Mixing and aeration are achieved simultaneously either by pumping air through porous ceramic diffuser tiles (or domes) spaced at frequent intervals along the base of the aeration tank, or by using mechanical surface aerators where paddles introduce air rather in the manner of an egg whisk. Diffused air systems

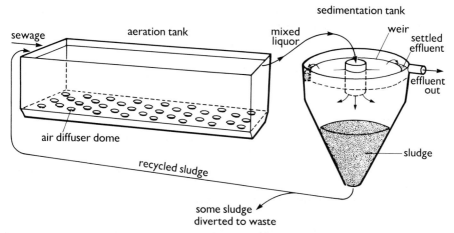

Fig 5.3 Diagrammatic representation of a typical diffused-air activated-sludge plant.

primarily aerate and secondarily mix whilst surface aerators primarily mix and secondarily aerate. However, whatever method is used, the objectives of thorough mixing of the sewage and sludge solids and aeration are the same.

A concentration of dissolved oxygen of about 1.0 mg l^{-1} must be maintained to achieve complete carbonaceous oxidation by the heterotrophic bacteria and about 2 mg l^{-1} is necessary for nitrification to occur. The respiratory rate of activated sludge is relatively independent of dissolved oxygen concentration down to the former concentration and the growth of nitrifying bacteria is not limited above the latter concentration. Thus it is uneconomical and of no advantage to maintain oxygen concentrations in excess of 2 mg l^{-1}. They should not however be allowed to fall below 0.5 mg l^{-1} for carbonaceous oxidation and 2 mg l^{-1} for nitrification.

After several hours' aeration, the mixture of activated sludge and treated sewage (mixed liquor) overflows into a large sedimentation tank (also called settling and separating tanks) where under quiescent conditions any solids capable of doing so settle to the bottom whilst the purified effluent overflows at the surface via a weir. Some of the sludge solids which are pumped from the base of the sedimentation tank are diverted as waste but most are returned back to the aeration tank to be mixed again with the inflowing sewage. Most activated-sludge plants in Britain are operated to maintain between 2000 and 6000 mg l^{-1} suspended solids in the mixed liquor of the aeration tank. The settled activated sludge has a highly water-retentive, gel-like structure and the recycled slurry normally contains between 0.5 and 2.0 per cent dry solids. It is extremely difficult to consolidate the sludge beyond about 4 per cent dry solids by the use of gravity alone.

There are several distinct purification steps in the whole process but these are masked by the mixing and are difficult to recognise. However, experimental work has shown that on mixing returned sludge with settled sewage there is a rapid uptake of some components in the waste by the sludge flocs. This is shown by the rapid reduction in the BOD_5 of the waste water. It is generally agreed that this initial rapid removal is due to the adsorption of soluble materials and flocculation of colloidal materials by the sludge floc surfaces. Some of the soluble organic matter is immediately oxidised, as indicated by the increase of respiration rate by the organisms in the sludge solids when fresh settled sewage is added. Other less biodegradable materials are oxidised more slowly. As the organic substrates in the water are used up there is a decline in respiratory rate so that at the aeration tank outlet the rate of respiration is only one-tenth that at the inlet. During the early stages when rapid oxidation is taking place the bacteria are synthesising cellular material but, if aeration is continued in the absence of substrate, the organisms oxidise their cellular contents and respire at the minimum level necessary to maintain the cell viable. This is known as **endogenous respiration** and is vital to the efficiency of the process since it reduces the amount of sludge produced, which has to be disposed of, and it provides the time needed for the flocculated organic solids to be oxidised before the sludge is ready to treat further quantities.

The aeration tanks of many activated-sludge plants are long, deep and narrow channels operating on the 'plug-flow' or 'piston-flow' principle. However, there are some completely mixed aeration tanks in operation which, at least in theory, immediately mix the total contents of the aeration tank with inflowing fresh settled sewage and returned sludge. This instantaneously dilutes the waste water and has advantages in that sudden strong doses of either organic material or toxic waste are reduced. Plug-flow systems can be simply regarded as an infinite number of completely mixed reactors connected in series so that instantaneous mixing of the total tank contents does not occur.

Basic biology   The activated-sludge process is a completely aquatic system, in contrast with biological filters where some areas of the film receive the direct flow of waste water while others remain dry but surrounded by air at 100 per cent humidity. Between these extremes there are many different degrees of moisture content providing a great variety of habitats for animal, plant and microbial life. However, the completely aquatic nature of the activated-sludge process means that only aquatic organisms can survive and this results in a much less varied fauna and flora. As with other biological oxidation-treatment processes, the activated-sludge process ultimately depends on the metabolic activities of micro-organisms which utilise the organic waste both as a respiratory substrate and as a material for cell synthesis.

Activated-sludge solids are composed of flocculated masses of bacteria and colloidal organic matter to which ciliated protozoa attach. About 30 per cent of the sludge mass is composed of bacteria and, as in biological filters, many are Gram-negative genera. Cytological examination of activated-sludge floc indicates that it is generally composed of aggregations of small rod-shaped bacteria, surrounded by a gel-like material, so giving the classical zoogloeal appearance. Flocculation is essential in the activated-sludge process for separating the solids from effluent in the sedimentation tank. However, sedimentation itself acts as a selective pressure for those organisms that will survive in the process since it is only the settleable organisms that are returned back to the aeration tank; others are washed out in the effluent. There are many theories as to why bacteria flocculate. Much information has been derived from laboratory cultures but a great deal more is needed from work carried out on organisms in real systems.

Under the microscope the sludge can be seen as discrete pieces or flocs. The size and physical structure of the flocs are important parameters since they influence the settling properties of the sludge in the sedimentation tank. A major operational problem with the activated-sludge process is the phenomenon known as **bulking** in which the sludge becomes difficult to settle. As a result some may be discharged in the effluent which considerably reduces its quality. At the same time, appreciable quantities of sludge may be lost from the system. Although some causes of bulking are known, such as organic overloading, under-aeration and sudden increased loadings of carbonaceous wastes, the phenomenon is still not fully understood.

Fungi are not normally found as dominant organisms in the activated-sludge process, except for the occasional occurrence of heavy growths of predaceous fungi which prey upon nematodes, rotifers and protozoa. However, when growth of bacteria is inhibited by industrial discharge abundant growths of fungi may replace them, as can happen if the pH is reduced by acid from plating works. In general the appearance of fungi in activated sludge is associated with industrial effluent present in the sewage. When they flourish the fungi adversely affect the settling properties of the sludge.

Most macro-invertebrates are not present in activated-sludge systems but protozoa, nematodes, rotifers and the annelid worm *Aelosoma* are often observed. Protozoa are plentiful in the activated-sludge process and populations of 50 000 cells per millilitre are commonly reported in the mixed liquor. Very little is known about the role of the other microscopic animals such as rotifers and nematodes. They are usually in small numbers and are unlikely to play a major role in the processes. There is not even circumstantial evidence to suggest that their presence or absence is associated with either effluent quality or settling qualities of the sludge.

Rotating biological contactors (RBCs)

The use of spaced vertical discs as partially submerged contact surfaces has been known for about 50 years but it was not until the 1960s that the role of the discs, known as **rotating biological contactors** (**RBCs**),

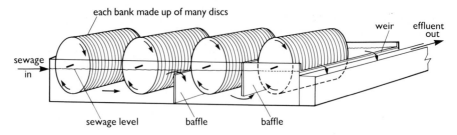

each bank made up of many discs

weir   effluent out

sewage in

sewage level   baffle   baffle

Fig 5.4 Diagrammatic representation of a train of rotating biological contactors as typically used in the USA.

was seriously investigated. By 1965 the system had become fairly well established in Europe and by 1969 was successfully operating in 200 sites, mainly in Germany and Austria but also in France and Switzerland. Subsequently plants of this type were introduced into the USA and the UK for the treatment of sewage from small, isolated communities.

In many ways RBCs resemble biological filters but they also have some of the characteristics of an activated-sludge plant. As with filters the microbial biomass is attached to the surfaces of the reactor, that is to say it is a fixed-film reactor, but it differs significantly in that the surfaces take the form of discs which rotate at axle depth in a flow of sewage. As each part of the disc spends half its time submerged in sewage and half its time in the air, the film is kept both aerobic and in contact with the sewage. Like activated sludge this process is completely aquatic and it follows that only aquatic fauna and flora develop.

The basic outline of the process is shown in fig 5.4. Settled sewage travels along a channel fitted with baffles to prevent short-circuiting and to induce plug-flow conditions. Large discs (up to about 4 m in diameter) of either plastic or metal mesh, mounted upon a common axle rod, rotate at about 1 r.p.m., partially submerged in the sewage flow. Usually, banks of discs are mounted with their axles at right angles to the flow, but in other cases the axles may be parallel to the flow. There are usually several banks of discs spaced at regular intervals down the length of the sewage channel. Discs may be mechanically driven by chains and cogs or assisted, and sometimes totally driven, by air which is pumped through the sewage into the banks of discs which act like paddle wheels. The discs are not usually completely flat but perforated and corrugated to provide as much surface area as possible for the biological film. The major advantage of this process is that it conserves energy. For this reason the use of such plants became popular in the USA during the energy crisis of the late 1970s and early 1980s although RBCs still tend to serve the smaller towns rather than large towns and cities.

One other economic advantage of this type of plant is that there is a negligible loss of head of liquid passing through the system. Furthermore the retention time and flow pattern is more controllable than for a biological filter, where controlled channeling of the flow results in a certain amount of sewage passing through in a shorter time than desired. Another advantage is that all surfaces are completely wetted. These factors together normally result in the disc filter being more efficient than an equivalent-sized biological filter.

Basic biology   As in other secondary biological-treatment processes the film consists primarily of bacteria, some fungi, many protozoa and a few metazoa such as rotifers, nematodes and the annelid worm *Aelosoma*. However, this is a relatively new process and less is known about its biology than that of other secondary treatment systems, although there is every reason to expect that the bacterial and fungal populations will closely resemble those found in activated-sludge plants and percolating filters.

More is known about the protozoan and metazoan populations. The species found closely mirror those of activated-sludge plants. As in the activated-sludge process, there is an absence of the macro-invertebrate populations associated with biological filters and this should be expected since RBCs are aquatic rather than semi-aquatic systems.

The reed bed treatment process

The first full-scale trial of this method was undertaken in Germany in 1974 and proved so successful that the plant was expanded to deal with a population of up to 10 000. The key feature of the root zone method is that a bed of rhizomes of the reed *Phragmites* provides an hydraulic pathway through which the waste water flows. This pathway (**rhizosphere**) is the annular space between rhizomes, roots and the surrounding soil. The movement of the mesh of roots, rhizomes and soil prevents clogging of the rhizosphere. The reeds provide atmospheric oxygen to the rhizosphere via the leaves, stems, roots and rhizomes. The waste water is therefore treated aerobically by bacterial activity in the rhizosphere but also anaerobically in the surrounding soil.

In addition to treating sewage it is possible to compost sludges aerobically above ground level in a layer of straw derived from the dead leaves and stems of the reeds. This novel process has been known for about 20 years but was introduced into Britain in 1985. There are now some 16 **reed beds** in England, most of which serve small, rural communities of between 25 and 1260 people.

Fig 5.5 shows the basic features of a reed bed. Existing soil is removed from the site to a depth of about 1½ metres below the depth of the sewage flow and sealed with clay, synthetic fabric or asphalt to retain water and to prevent contamination of the groundwater. After sealing the site, the soil into which the reeds are to be planted is placed into the vacant hole. The filler can be local soil provided it has some quartz and chalk with a calcium content of 2000–2500 mg kg^{-1}. Chalk can be added to achieve this. Alternatively the bed can be filled with pea gravel. In all cases the bed is

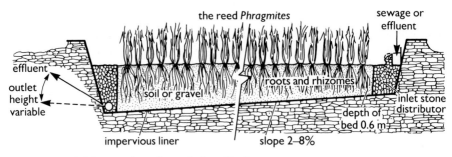

Fig 5.5 Section through a typical reed bed.

filled to a depth of 0.6 m, avoiding the use of heavy vehicles and machinery which might compress the planting medium and reduce its hydraulic conductivity. The inlet and outlet ends of the bed are provided with trenches filled with stones, granite or slag which help to achieve an even distribution of waste water to the bed. The outlet is via a pipe whose level can be varied so that the water level in the bed can be raised or lowered.

For the successful growth of *Phragmites* it is essential for the soil to remain waterlogged, but not necessarily covered with water, for most of the year. As mature reeds transpire and evaporate about 1500 mm of water annually it is important to have an adequate supply of water. Usually rhizomes of the reed are planted in a new bed and it takes about three years before the bed matures sufficiently to become fully operational. Seeds can be used but the maturation period is then extended by a further year. At first mainly fresh water is supplied to the bed but as time goes on and the reeds become established, sewage can be added in increasing concentrations. After three years sewage can be applied without dilution.

There are several advantages in the use of reed beds. They are simple and cheap to construct, operate and maintain while giving a consistent effluent quality over a wide range of conditions. They are environmentally acceptable since they merge with the surrounding countryside and, indeed, offer local wildlife considerable conservation potential. The main disadvantage is the time taken to reach full maturity.

Basic biology   While quite a lot is known about the reeds, little work has been carried out on the microbial processes which take place within the bed. It is certainly known that a mixture of aerobic and anaerobic processes take place and it must be expected that the bacterial populations will be similar to those found in other more conventional processes. Protozoa are known to occur in some, but not all, reed beds but it is not yet clear which are the major groups represented and what effects the presence or absence of protozoa might have upon the quality of the effluent.

Oxidation ponds

Oxidation ponds are classified as a type of waste stabilisation pond or lagoon but, unlike some of the other types of pond included under that general heading, oxidation ponds rely upon algae as their source of oxygen. Certain other waste stabilisation ponds, such as aeration lagoons, are kept aerobic by mechanical means and others, such as anaerobic ponds or lagoons, have no input of oxygen at all.

There are three basic types of oxidation pond: firstly the facultative pond which is aerobic in the upper layers where light penetrates but anaerobic at the bottom; secondly the high-rate aerobic lagoon which is shallow, its high concentration of algae and mechanical mixing keeping the entire contents aerobic; and thirdly the maturation pond or lagoon which is used for tertiary treatment when a high-quality effluent is required. Maturation ponds will be dealt with later in this chapter under tertiary treatment processes.

Most waste stabilisation ponds are facultative oxidation ponds and are commonly used for the full treatment of crude sewage or industrial organic waste waters without sedimentation. They are characterised by having an upper aerobic zone and a lower anaerobic zone, active purification processes occurring in both. In the aerobic zone the processes are the same as those in the other aerobic sewage treatments. In the anaerobic zone the organic matter is broken down by anaerobic bacteria to produce gases such as methane, nitrogen and carbon dioxide. The facultative oxidation pond is the only secondary treatment process in which anaerobic decomposition plays a significant role, with approximately 20–30 per cent of the BOD_5 load being lost as gas to the atmosphere.

Oxidation ponds are very different from biological filters and activated-sludge plants in that they rely upon light as a source of energy in order to keep the process aerobic via the photosynthetic activities of the abundant green algae that are present. As light cannot penetrate far into sewage, the ponds need to be shallow and this requires large areas of land. For comparison the sewage derived from a population of 1000 people needs areas of 35 m^2, 210 m^2 and 2000 m^2 when treated by activated sludge, biological filters and oxidation ponds respectively. The figure of 2000 m^2 in fact refers to ideal climatic conditions, as in the tropics. In areas with temperate climates and seasonal ice cover, up to 50 000 m^2 is needed. However, the sewage does not need to undergo primary sedimentation and requires less frequent and skilled attention than the other two processes. For these reasons waste stabilisation ponds are almost exclusively restricted to regions with sunny climates, a lot of available land and cheap, unskilled labour.

Basic biology The anaerobic activities of the lower layers are carried out by anaerobic bacteria and the organisms and processes are very similar to those which occur in anaerobic digesters, to be described under tertiary treatment processes later. Little is really known about the biology of the upper aerobic layers of facultative oxidation ponds. The dominant organisms appear to be similar to those found in other aerobic processes with *Pseudomonas*, *Flavobacterium* and *Achromobacter* being the dominant bacteria.

Fungi have been isolated but do not appear to be of major significance. It has been suggested that they are restricted because of the high pH caused by the algae. Similarly the heterotrophic protozoa have not yet been credited with a significant role in the process and removal of bacteria has so far been attributed to filter-feeding cladoceran crustacea. However, large numbers of ciliated protozoa are found in these ponds and it is likely that protozoa are of importance. It is the lack of research on these processes that results in our present, perhaps unbalanced, view.

Although bacteria are the prime agents of organic degradation in the ponds, the oxygen essential for the aerobic processes is mostly supplied by the photosynthetic activity of the phototrophic algae and protozoa. The most commonly recorded genera of algae include *Chlorella, Scenedesmus, Chlamydomonas, Micractinium, Euglena, Ankistrodesmus, Oscillatoria* and *Microcystis*. Dominance within these algae varies throughout the year. They have different powers of oxygenation and *Chlorella* and *Scenedesmus* are considered the most productive. In addition to their oxygenating properties algae also remove plant nutrients such as phosphorus and nitrogen. This is achieved partly by direct nutrient uptake and partly as a result of the pH change induced by reduction of carbon dioxide concentration as a result of photosynthesis. This causes phosphates to precipitate.

Facultative oxidation ponds also support a large macro-invertebrate population including chironomid larvae, nematode and tubificid worms in the lower deoxygenated sludge layer, and a large zooplankton population including rotifers, and cladocera and copepod crustacea. Which population becomes established depends to some extent on the retention time of the pond. Crustaceans, for example, only become well established in ponds with retention times of more than 10 days. The crustacea most commonly recorded include *Daphnia, Moina* and *Cyclops* and these play a major role in the removal of excess algae which would otherwise add to the effluent's BOD_5.

Tertiary treatment

Secondary treatment results in the separation of two fractions, effluent and solids. Any further treatment of these two fractions is called tertiary treatment. Should the effluent be entering a water course which is to be used as a source of potable water then it may undergo 'polishing' to remove further suspended particulate material. This may be carried out chemically and mechanically using flocculating agents and microstraining devices, or biologically in a maturation pond. Solids derived from primary and secondary processes are most frequently treated in an anaerobic digester which will be described later.

Maturation ponds

These have already been mentioned briefly in the section concerning oxidation ponds. They differ from facultative oxidation ponds in that they receive a much lower organic load, since they deal with effluents after secondary treatment, and are much more likely to remain completely aerobic. However, like facultative oxidation ponds, they are shallow unmixed lagoons in which algae maintain aerobic conditions. Most of the organic carbon has already been removed by secondary treatment but inevitably some further removal takes place in the maturation pond. Improvement of the effluents is not by soluble carbon removal but by the removal of suspended solids, reduction in the number of enteric bacteria present, and reduction in nitrate and phosphate concentrations. Algae remain suspended in the effluent after treatment and add to the BOD_5 of the final effluent.

Basic biology Coliform bacteria reductions of well over 90 per cent are generally recorded in all geographical regions including the UK. Sunlight is said to be the major factor which removes coliforms but no one has yet examined the potential role of protozoa in this process, although their presence in high numbers is well established. The removal of nitrogen and phosphorus is brought about in maturation ponds as a result of algal and bacterial activities. Some direct removal of nitrogen occurs by algal uptake but the majority is probably due to denitrification by bacteria. Similarly, while some phosphate removal is by direct algal uptake most is removed by precipitation brought about by high pH values resulting from algal photosynthesis. Several algae have been recorded in maturation ponds including diatoms, such as *Stephanodiscus* and *Nitzschia*, and chlorophytes, such as *Chlamydomonas*, *Heteromastix*, *Chlorella*, *Scenedesmus* and *Cryptomonas*. High concentrations not only add to the BOD_5 of the effluent but also prevent the penetration of sunlight which reduces the mortality rates of coliform bacteria. The algal populations are kept in check by cladoceran crustacea such as *Cyclops*, *Daphnia*, *Bosmina* and *Simocephalus*, and it has been proposed that the crustacea be harvested as a commercial product as food for fish in aquaria.

Cladocera commonly occur in maturation ponds provided the retention time is sufficiently long (10–12 days). Fish such as carp, roach, chub and perch are also sometimes cultivated in maturation ponds but there are several problems. While the fish grow at economic rates they are prone to disease and difficult to harvest. Their presence also affects the algae which increase significantly and affect effluent quality. This is due to the predation of the fish upon the zooplankton of crustacea and rotifers which feed on the algae.

Anaerobic treatment processes

Several uncontrolled anaerobic processes take place during the treatment of sewage and organic industrial waste waters. For example **denitrification**, that is the conversion of nitrite and nitrate into gaseous nitrogen, can take place during the sedimentation of activated sludge if anaerobic conditions prevail in the settlement tank. Similarly sulphate in sewage may be reduced to form hydrogen sulphide in sewers. This escapes into the atmosphere and becomes biologically oxidised to sulphuric acid on the damp walls of the sewer. Such reactions cause problems. Nitrogen formation in the sedimentation tank causes 'sludge rise' when nitrogen bubbles caught in the sludge floc make it rise to the surface and overflow into the effluent. Hydrogen sulphide is highly toxic and sulphuric acid rapidly attacks concrete. The occurrence of anaerobic biological reactions depends firstly on the presence of the appropriate bacteria and secondly upon the redox (oxidation–reduction) potential being poised in the correct range long enough for the bacteria to grow.

Not all anaerobic processes are uncontrolled. Indeed sometimes plants are constructed with the object of denitrifying effluents, that is removing nitrates, before discharge into a water course used as a source of drinking water. However, the most widely used anaerobic process is called **anaerobic digestion**, **sludge digestion** or just **digestion**.

Solids derived from primary sedimentation, excess activated sludge and sloughed solids from biological filters are bulky slurries from which it is difficult to remove water (**dewater**). Since approximately one-third of the costs of treating sewage are attributable to the disposal of solids it is obviously important to reduce their bulk as far as possible, and this is usually carried out by anaerobic digestion followed by dewatering. Some early anaerobic digesters, e.g. Imhoff tanks, combined primary sedimentation and digestion, but in modern sewage works digestion is separated from primary sedimentation. Digestion is either carried out at ambient temperatures in large, open tanks or lagoons or more commonly at about 35°C in heated covered tanks. The rate at which the former 'cold' digesters work largely depends on the ambient temperature and overall residence times can be up to 12 months. This is far too long for sewage works serving large towns and cities. At the larger sewage works heated digesters are more commonly used and the methane derived from the process is used as a power source for the work's generators.

During digestion not only is methane (biogas) produced but the organic carbon content is reduced by about 25 per cent and, although the suspended solids content is only increased by about 3 per cent, it is easier to dewater. After digestion is completed the solids are pumped to drying beds for dewatering or direct to ships for disposal at sea. While this is still common practice in the UK, European legislation is likely to prevent, or at least limit, the dumping of sewage sludge at sea in the future. Other methods such as incineration will take its place. Dried sludge derived entirely from domestic sewage can be bagged and sold as fertiliser. However, the presence of industrial waste often precludes this because of contamination by heavy metals which adsorb on to solids during primary sedimentation.

Basic biology Anaerobic digestion is almost exclusively carried out by bacteria. Although anaerobic protozoa have been found in Imhoff tanks almost nothing is known about the presence, distribution and role of these organisms in anaerobic digesters. The essential feature of anaerobic digestion is the presence of methanogenic (methane-producing) bacteria which ferment organic substrates such as acetate, methanol, formate, formaldehyde and carbon dioxide to convert them into methane. Methanogenic bacteria naturally occur in anaerobic sediments in ponds and rivers and also in the rumens of herbivorous mammals.

However, the complete digestion process is far more complicated than simple methane production. It takes place in three stages, though there is considerable interaction between the first two stages. The first stage is the anaerobic hydrolysis of proteins, fats and polysaccharides to produce amino acids and short-chain peptides, long-chain fatty acids and glycerol, and monosaccharides and disaccharides respectively. The major bacteria hydrolysing protein are anaerobic spore-formers including *Clostridium* spp., while those hydrolysing fats include *Micrococcus* sp., *Bacillus* sp., *Streptomyces* sp., *Alcaligenes* sp. and *Pseudomonas* sp. Anaerobic cellulolytic bacteria (motile, Gram-negative rods) and organisms capable of hydrolysing hemi-cellulose (*Bacteroides ruminicola*) have also been isolated from digesters.

The second stage involves the fermentation of the products of stage 1 with the production of volatile fatty acids – particularly acetic (ethanoic) acid, alcohols, aldehydes, ketones, ammonia, carbon dioxide, hydrogen and water. This is carried out principally by a number of obligate anaerobes although some facultative anaerobes may also play a part. The final stage is methanogenesis whereby the products of the second stage are converted into methane, carbon dioxide and water by obligate anaerobes such as *Methanobacterium* spp., *Methanobacillus* sp., etc.

6

Protozoology of the processes

Protozoa occur in all biological sewage and potable water-treatment processes. Although the methods used often differ markedly from one another, the protozoan populations have a great degree of similarity and some species are common to all processes. The presence of protozoa in biological water-treatment processes was noted almost as soon as each process was introduced, but it is only in recent years that the significance of these organisms has begun to emerge. Much of the early work was concerned with the description of the fauna in these habitats but this was followed by a period when several workers attempted to relate the species or communities of protozoa to effluent quality and plant performance. That approach is also to be followed in this chapter where an outline comparative description of the protozoan fauna in all processes precedes a discussion of their ecology and role in individual systems.

The protozoan fauna of water- and sewage-treatment processes

Protozoa found in water-treatment systems

Groundwaters were once believed to be pristine – without bacteria and protozoa. Recent discoveries have shown this to be untrue; bacteria are found in all groundwater and protozoa, particularly colourless flagellates and amoebae, have also been found. However, there are much greater numbers in water-treatment processes.

The list of protozoa found in slow sand filters included in table 6.1 shows that there are many differences between the faunas of water- and sewage-treatment processes. Perhaps we should expect this since there are great differences between sewage and the water used as a source for drinking-

Table 6.1. *Some protozoa commonly found in water- and sewage-treatment processes.* * = *commonly found,* 0 = *recorded but not common,* — = *not recorded. Filt = biological filter; A-S = activated sludge; RBC = rotating biological contactor; Oxid = oxidation lagoon and S-SF = slow sand filter*

Protozoan species	Saprobity	Filt	A-S	RBC	Oxid	S-SF
Flagellates						*
Bodo spp.	p-α	*	0	*	*	—
Pleuromonas jaculans	p-α	*	0	*	0	—
Euglena spp.	p-α	*	—	—	*	0
Peranema trichophorum	p-M	*	*	*	*	—
Choanoflagellates	—	—	—	—	—	*
Amoebae						*
Amoeba proteus	β	0	0	*	*	—
Acanthamoeba castellanii	—	0	0	0	*	—
Hartmanella sp.	—	0	0	0	*	—
Naegleria sp.	—	0	0	0	*	—
Arcella vulgaris	—	*	*	*	—	—
Centropyxis aculeata	—	—	—	*	—	—
Euglypha sp.	β	0	0	—	—	*
Ciliates						
Trachelophyllum pusillum	β	0	*	*	0	0
Hemiophrys fusidens	p-β	0	*	*	*	0
Amphileptus claparedei	α	0	*	*	0	—
Litonotus fasciola	α	*	*	*	*	*
Trochilia minuta	β	*	0	*	—	—
Chilodonella uncinata	α	*	0	*	—	*
Cyclidium spp.	α	*	0	0	0	*
Glaucoma scintillans	p	*	0	0	0	*
Cinetochilum margaritaceum	β	*	0	*	—	*
Carchesium polypinum	p-M	*	*	*	*	—
Zoothamnium sp.	β	0	0	*	—	0
Vorticella campanula	o-β	0	0	0	—	*
Vorticella convallaria	M	*	*	*	*	*
Vorticella microstoma	p-α	*	*	*	*	0
Vorticella striata	o	*	*	0	—	—
Epistylis plicatilis	M	0	0	*	—	0
Opercularia spp.	α	*	*	*	—	0
Aspidisca cicada	p-β	0	*	*	0	*
Euplotes spp.	M	0	*	0	—	0
Stylonychia spp.	M	0	0	0	*	*
Tachysoma pellionella	β	0	0	0	—	*

water supplies, particularly of concentration rather than composition. Sewage contains far greater concentrations of organic nutrients and bacteria than abstracted water, which results in lower populations of micro-organisms in slow sand filters. The species are apparently different too. There are few data available, but flagellated protozoa and naked amoebae are reported to be commonly present although they remain to be identified even as genera. Choanoflagellates, most uncommon in sewage-treatment processes, are said to be common in slow sand filters. Surprisingly the ciliates found tend to be those found associated with α-mesosaprobic conditions. This is unexpected since the organic loading of a slow sand filter is generally rather low and it is not usual practice to abstract water from heavily polluted sources.

Protozoa found in sewage-treatment processes

Protozoa are plentiful in all the sewage-treatment processes mentioned previously but are more abundant in aerobic sewage-treatment processes than anaerobic processes. For example, it is common to find numbers in the order of 50 000 cells per millilitre in the mixed liquor of an activated-sludge plant. Calculations based on such numbers indicate that protozoa can constitute approximately 5 per cent of the dry weight of the suspended solids in the aeration tank. More than 400 species of protozoa occur in sewage-treatment processes and some of the more commonly found ones are listed in table 6.1.

Flagellated protozoa are often reported to be present; they may be found in sewage or in the processes themselves. They are usually colourless and either feed on bacteria or compete with them for soluble organic compounds. The zooflagellate *Bodo* is frequently found in sewage and at the top of biological filters. Green phytoflagellates, such as *Euglena* spp., are commonly found in oxidation lagoons, in the upper layers of slow sand filters and occasionally at the top of biological filters where light is available. Their close relative *Peranema trichophorum*, which feeds upon bacteria, is found in similar habitats to those of *Bodo*.

The amoebae are represented both by the naked and testate forms. Little work has been carried out on the identification of naked amoebae in these processes. They are usually present in low numbers but can, on occasion, become dominant. The testate amoebae are easier to recognise than naked amoebae; *Arcella vulgaris* and *Centropyxis aculeata*, both of which produce organic shells, are commonly reported in small numbers but *Euglypha* sp., with its siliceous shell, is less common. Testate amoebae have low rates of growth and are usually only noticed during the summer months in plants operating at low sewage flow rates.

The ciliated protozoa are nearly always numerically the dominant protozoa in sewage-treatment processes and usually represented by the greatest variety of species. Most of the ciliates feed on bacteria but some are carnivores, feeding upon other ciliates. A few ingest algae and sometimes filamentous growths. A total of about 250 species of ciliate have been reported in sewage-treatment processes, of which perhaps only a third are commonly found. Since there are about 10 000 species that could inhabit these processes, it is obvious that some form of ecological selection is involved. There is a high preponderence of those species which are closely associated with surfaces and normally either attach themselves to the sludge floc or microbial film by means of a stalk, as with the peritrichous

Table 6.2. *Eight most important protozoa in biological filters and activated-sludge plants in the UK. The values in columns 1 and 2 give the order of importance, where 1 indicates most important species and 0 unimportant. In columns 3 and 4 B = bactivorous, C = carnivorous, F = able to ingest filamentous organisms, Sed = sedentary, Crl = crawling and FSw = free-swimming*

Ciliate species	Filter	Act-Slg	Food	Habit
Opercularia microdiscum	1	0	B	Sed
Carchesium polypinum	2	7	B	Sed
Vorticella convallaria	3	2	B	Sed
Chilodonella uncinata	4	0	F	Crl
Opercularia coarctata	5	5	B	Sed
Opercularia phryganeae	6	0	B	Sed
Vorticella striata	7	0	B	Sed
Aspidisca cicada	8	1	B	Crl
Vorticella microstoma	0	3	B	Sed
Trachelophyllum pusillum	0	4	C	FSw
Vorticella alba	0	6	B	Sed
Euplotes moebiusi	0	8	B	Crl

ciliates *Vorticella, Carchesium, Zoothamnium, Epistylis* and *Opercularia*, or crawl over surfaces as do the hypotrichous ciliates *Aspidisca* spp. and *Euplotes* spp. Those ciliates which are normally free swimming in the liquid phase also occur in activated-sludge plants and biological filters but are far more common in the surface waters of oxidation lagoons.

It will be seen from table 6.1 that the protozoan fauna of biological filters, activated-sludge plants and RBCs have many species in common. There are more species simultaneously present in filters and RBCs and this is probably due to the greater variety of habitats that fixed-film reactors offer. The faunas of oxidation lagoons and reed beds are rather different and this probably reflects the difference between the former three totally aerobic systems and the latter two which are at least partially anaerobic. Oxidation lagoons and reed beds appear to have species most usually associated with poly- to α-mesosaprobic conditions (see chapter 3, page 32) although there are few data available to support this as a generalisation.

A major survey of protozoa from activated-sludge plants and biological filters in the UK was carried out in the 1970s to define which protozoa were most frequently found in these two aerobic processes. Since the abundance of an organism is often taken as an indicator of its importance in the ecology of a habitat, it was possible, using both abundance and frequency data, to identify those protozoa likely to be of greatest importance in biological filters and activated-sludge plants. A list of these is shown in table 6.2.

There are several general points to be made from the list. All the most important protozoa found in the two processes are ciliates. Most of them are sedentary, attaching themselves directly to the microbial films by means of a stalk. A few are crawling forms. All are known to feed on bacteria. The frequent presence of *Chilodonella* in filters may be of significance; this ciliate has the ability to engulf filamentous bacteria and algae which are more common in biological filters than in activated sludge.

The protozoan populations of all the processes are dynamic. The species continually change, as do the numbers of individuals, often on a day-to-day basis. Some of these changes are still not understood but others are regular and follow predictable patterns.

Spatial distribution

There must always be a definite sequence of environmental changes throughout a process, otherwise the quality of the effluent leaving the plant would be the same as the sewage entering. In processes where the microbial film is held in a static position with respect to the flow of liquid (fixed-film reactors such as biological filters, rotating biological contactors, reed beds and slow sand filters) different organisms thrive in different positions. For example, as sewage passes through the depth of a biological filter it is purified by microbial action so that conditions at the top are very different from those at the bottom. Different protozoan populations are found at the top of a filter compared to those below.

In an activated-sludge plant the situation is very different. Both the sewage and the microbial film or sludge floc flow down the aeration tank together and the organisms live in an ever-changing environment. After a period of low dissolved oxygen concentration in the sedimentation tank, they are recirculated to be mixed with fresh sewage in the aeration tank. If fixed substrata, such as glass microscope slides, are introduced into the aeration tank at various intervals along its length different protozoa colonise the slides and some of these are different to those growing upon the sludge floc.

Different organisms tend to predominate at different levels in a biological filter, for example the metazoa favour the lower levels while the protozoa favour the upper ones. However the protozoa also vary with depth. There is a restricted protozoa fauna at the surface which changes to one of greater species variety further down. Amoebae and flagellates are most commonly found in the surface levels while ciliated protozoa occur further down.

The vertical stratification of organisms in a filter depends on many interrelated factors which are extremely difficult to unravel. However, generally there is a change from those species in the surface layers which utilise soluble organic substrates, to those in the middle which feed on bacteria, to those at the bottom which feed upon ciliates. The organisms appear to respond to changes in the relative abundance of different forms of food supply. However, this is only part of the picture. The most common explanation for the vertical distribution of protozoa in filters is their association with the different levels of saprobity (chapter 3, page 32) found there. Gradual purification of sewage takes place during its passage through the filter so that polysaprobic conditions and associated species occur at the top followed by mesosaprobic conditions of diminishing intensities with their appropriate species towards the base. The same phenomena are to be found in rotating biological contactors where the discs near to the sewage inlet carry film dominated by polysaprobic species while those close to the effluent carry meso- and oligosaprobic species. Similarly one could expect to find comparable changes in the protozoan populations in oxidation ponds and perhaps also in reed beds although they have not yet been reported in the literature. In slow sand filters the protozoa are concentrated in the top 1–2 cm layer and the population decreases exponentially downwards and is more or less absent below about 25 cm. This is probably due to bacteria being removed by predation in the top levels, leaving very few for those organisms deeper down.

The zones in biological filters, RBCs and slow sand filters, however, are not static. They move up and down in response to the organic and hydraulic loadings applied. For example, the polysaprobic zone in a biological filter will extend further down should the organic loading be increased until perhaps the microbial biomass increases to improve the effluent quality. It is changes such as these which have led some researchers to believe that it is possible to monitor effluent quality from a knowledge of the protozoan populations.

Temporal succession

As indicated above, spatial zonation of protozoa does not occur in activated-sludge plants since the microbial film carrying the protozoa moves with the liquid. It is continually mixed and recirculated, after sedimentation, into the aeration tank. However, similar to the succession of different protozoan types in ponds and streams during self-purification, there is a succession of protozoan types during the maturation of activated sludge. When a plant is first started up there is little sludge present and purification is only partially achieved. As time goes on sludge grows and accumulates and the effluent quality improves. A more or less predictable succession of protozoa appears in the plant during maturation as illustrated in fig 6.1.

Flagellates such as *Oicomonas* sp., *Heteronema* sp., *Peranema* sp. and *Bodo* sp. are the first dominant protozoa to appear. As the numbers of flagellates decrease they are slowly replaced by free-swimming ciliates such as *Uronema* and *Paramecium*; these reach a peak after about three weeks. They are then replaced by the crawling hypotrichous ciliates *Aspidisca* spp. followed by attached peritrichs such as *Vorticella, Epistylis* and *Opercularia*. If one compares the ciliate species in order of appearance in a developing sludge with their positions in the saprobic system, it will be seen that there is a tendency for polysaprobic species to occur in the early stages of development and for meso- and oligosaprobic species to occur in the later stages when a good quality effluent is obtained. Several explanations for such successions have been suggested, more or less following those

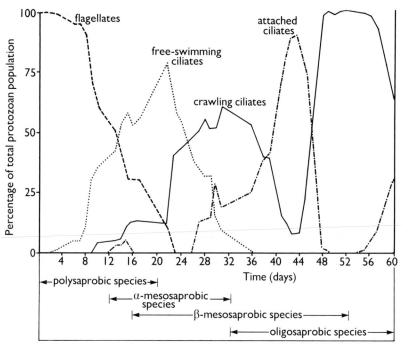

Fig 6.1 Graph illustrating the succession of dominant protozoa in a developing activated sludge. The lower portion indicates the periods when species of different saprobities were present.

proposed for the vertical stratification of protozoa in biological filters, that is a combination of nutritional preferences and saprobic condition. However, it is possible to obtain similar successions from computer simulations relying upon the growth kinetics, nutrition and settling properties of the organisms concerned without any consideration of saprobity. These model successions will be described in the next chapter.

The use of protozoa to indicate effluent quality

It is evident that spatial and temporal distributions, saprobity and final effluent quality are all interrelated. As stated above this has led to the proposal that protozoa be used to indicate the effluent quality. Early suggestions promoted the idea of using single species to indicate effluent quality but this has many disadvantages and now most agree that communities of protozoa must be used. A large-scale survey of activated-sludge plants in the UK during the 1970s indicated that there was a correlation between the species structure of activated sludge and the quality of the effluent. In order to test this hypothesis the effluents from the plants were divided into four categories according to their BOD_5: very high quality (BOD_5 range 0–10 mg 1^{-1}), high quality (11–20 mg 1^{-1}); inferior quality (21–30 mg 1^{-1}) and low quality (above 30 mg 1^{-1}). The frequencies of each

Table 6.3. *Percentage frequency of occurrence of some protozoa in plants producing effluents within the four ranges of BOD₅*

BOD₅ range	Frequency of occurrence (%) and point awarded (in brackets)			
(mg l⁻¹)	0–10	11–20	21–30	>30
Vorticella convallaria	63 (3)	73 (4)	37 (2)	22 (1)
Vorticella fromenteli	38 (5)	33 (4)	12 (1)	0 (0)
Carchesium polypinum	19 (3)	47 (5)	12 (2)	0 (0)
Aspidisca cicada	75 (3)	80 (3)	50 (2)	56 (2)
Euplotes patella	38 (4)	25 (3)	24 (3)	0 (0)
Flagellated protozoa	0 (0)	0 (0)	37 (4)	45 (6)

species occurring in plants delivering effluents in these four categories were calculated on a percentage basis. Some of the species were associated with all categories of effluent, but, as shown in table 6.3 there was a tendency for a given species to occur more frequently in plants delivering effluents within a particular effluent quality range. This indicated that the protozoan species found within the mixed liquor were in some way associated with effluent quality. It is evident from table 6.3 that *Carchesium polypinum*, for example, was found principally in plants which produced good quality effluent, whereas flagellated protozoa were restricted to plants producing inferior effluents.

An arbitrary total of 10 points was awarded to each species, and these were distributed between the four effluent categories so that the greatest number of points was given to the effluent category with which that species was most frequently associated. For example, a ciliate species occurring with frequencies of 60, 80, 40, and 20 per cent, in plants delivering effluent in the four categories, would be awarded the 10 points in the ratio of 6:8:4:2, that is, 3, 4, 2 and 1 respectively. Table 6.4 lists the frequencies of some species in plants delivering effluent in the four categories and illustrates the distribution of points for those species.

In order to predict the effluent quality of a particular plant the species of protozoa in the mixed liquor were identified and listed against the four effluent-quality categories. Using a comprehensive version of table 6.3 the appropriate number of points was awarded to each of the effluent categories for each species. The total number of points for each category was then calculated and that category receiving the highest total was the predicted effluent-quality category. The example in table 6.4 contains data originally obtained from a full-scale activated-sludge plant. It predicts an effluent BOD₅ of 0–10 mg l⁻¹ and was actually delivering a BOD₅ of 8 mg l⁻¹. Further surveys have revealed that this method gives the correct prediction in about 80 per cent of cases.

The problem with attempting to predict activated-sludge effluent quality is that the continual mixing and feedback of sludge often results in the

Table 6.4. *Example of the use of association ratings to predict the quality of effluent from an activated-sludge plant*

Protozoa in sludge	Effluent BOD_5 ranges (mg l^{-1})			
	0–10	11–20	21–30	>30
Trachelophyllum pusillum	3	3	3	1
Hemiophrys fusidens	3	4	3	0
Chilodonella cucullulus	4	4	1	1
Paramecium trichium	4	3	2	1
Vorticella communis	10	0	0	0
Vorticella convallaria	3	4	2	1
Vorticella fromenteli	5	4	1	0
Vorticella microstoma	2	4	2	2
Opercularia coarctata	2	2	4	2
Carchesium polypinum	3	5	2	0
Zoothamnium mucedo	10	0	0	0
Aspidisca cicada	3	3	2	2
Euplotes moebiusi	3	3	3	1
Euplotes affinis	6	4	0	0
Euplotes patella	4	3	3	0
Total points	65	46	28	11

survival of those protozoa which grow best under the most physiologically suitable situation found in the plant; usually the sedimentation tank. There is a much greater chance of success with fixed-film reactors since the organisms in them stratify into zones rather like the saprobic zones in a polluted river. However, percolating filters are very difficult to sample because of their construction. Taking a sample from a filter often results in digging it up which is detrimental to its operation. This is where RBCs have a distinct advantage. They are fixed-film reactors and are also constructed in such a way as to make sampling simple. Current research on RBCs seems likely to produce a good simple method to enable plant operators to predict effluent quality and general operational state from a knowledge of the protozoan fauna. It has already been possible to indicate that in some cases the hydraulic design of plant was not as good as it might be, simply because the protozoa were not found growing in the correct sequence. Later chemical tracer tests have demonstrated that this was indeed the case.

The role of protozoa in water-treatment processes

Very little work has been carried out on the role of protozoa in slow sand filters and this is probably due to their construction which makes it difficult to sample. However, most of the protozoa found in slow sand filters are known to feed upon bacteria. Experiments have shown, for example, that as the population of *Vorticella* spp. grows in the sand the numbers of viable (living) bacteria in the filtrate decrease. Similarly, observations on full-scale plants have demonstrated that there is an inverse relationship between the ciliate and flagellate protozoan populations and the numbers of viable bacteria emerging in the filtrate. No such relationship has been found between amoebae and bacterial populations even though it is known that amoebae prey upon bacteria. This evidence suggests that amoebae do not feed upon the dispersed bacteria which appear suspended in the filtrate but upon those which are attached to the surfaces of the sand grains. Further experimental work on laboratory-scale filters has shown that the addition of *Vorticella campanula* to protozoa-free filters has a significant beneficial effect upon filtrate quality with respect to its bacterial content.

The role of protozoa in sewage-treatment processes

While there is a large amount of information concerning the role of protozoa in the activated-sludge process, little work has been carried out on the role of these organisms in percolating filters, rotating biological contactors and oxidation lagoons. However, as there is a great deal of similarity between these aerobic processes it is reasonable to suppose that the protozoa play a similar role in each. No studies have been made on anaerobic processes.

Protozoa were originally thought to be harmful to the activated-sludge process. It was argued that, as they feed upon the bacterial populations, they inhibit microbial degradation processes. This has been shown to be untrue. Indeed, some evidence suggests that predation stimulates bacterial activity. All authorities now believe that protozoa play a vital role in the production of good quality effluents, but for a variety of reasons and to a variable extent. Considerable efforts to discover the role of these organisms were carried out in India during the 1940s. At that time it was even suggested that bacteria were of secondary importance in the purification processes since it was claimed that the colonial peritrichous ciliate *Epistylis* sp. in the absence of bacteria could account for 70 per cent reduction in the permanganate value, the albuminoid and ammoniacal nitrogen concentrations of sewage, and was also responsible for 80 per cent of the nitrification. Furthermore it was stated that without protozoa the sludge failed to grow and there was no clarification. Few of these claims have been substantiated and now most authorities agree that protozoa play a secondary but nonetheless important role in aerobic sewage-treatment processes.

Early workers attempted to assess the effects of protozoa in small-scale activated-sludge plants by selectively killing the protozoan populations. Although it was found that toluene treatment killed the protozoa and that there was a simultaneous deleterious effect upon effluent quality, such methods are open to much criticism since toluene is a highly toxic substance not only to protozoa but also to bacteria. Thus changes could be due to unintended effects upon bacterial populations. The better approach is to carry out the experiment in reverse and without the use of toxic substances. It is possible to construct small-scale plants which are totally

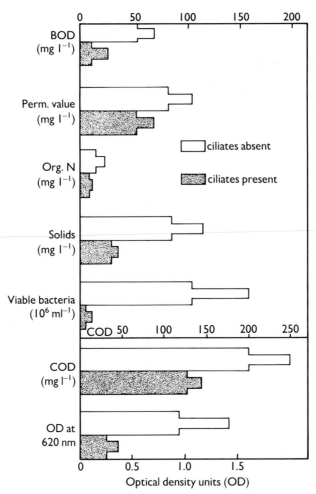

Fig 6.2 Bar chart of effluent quality issuing from laboratory-scale pilot plants operating in presence and absence of ciliated protozoa. The shoulders on the bars indicate ranges of variation between replicate plants.

closed from the atmosphere, sterilised and then inoculated with bacterial populations obtained from full-scale activated-sludge plants. Provided the plants are dosed with heat-treated sewage the sludges which grow can be kept free from protozoa. These methods made it possible for the first time to study the effect of the subsequent addition of protozoa and to quantify their effect upon effluent quality.

Under protozoa-free conditions plants produce highly turbid effluents of inferior quality and the turbidity is significantly related to the presence of very large numbers of bacteria suspended in the effluent (hundreds of millions ml^{-1}). Without protozoa the BOD_5 of the effluents are high as are

Fig 6.3 Photograph of effluents issuing from laboratory-scale pilot plants operating in the presence (+) and absence (−) of ciliated protozoa.

the contents of organic carbon, suspended solids and other parameters (fig 6.2). Cultures of ciliated protozoa can then be added to some plants while other replicates are kept operating under protozoa-free conditions as controls. After a few days, during which time the protozoan populations become properly established, there is a dramatic visual and chemical improvement in the effluent quality flowing from those plants containing protozoa. Clarity is greatly improved, which is associated with a significant decrease in the concentration of viable bacteria in the effluents. Furthermore, the effluent BOD_5 and concentrations of suspended solids and other factors decrease significantly. At the same time the control plants operating without protozoa continue to produce turbid effluents of lower quality. The bar chart in fig 6.2 illustrates the ranges of effluent qualities that may be obtained from small-scale pilot plants operating in the absence of ciliated protozoa and the photograph in fig 6.3 illustrates the appearance of the effluents three days after the addition of protozoa to three of the six replicate plants.

It seems clear from these results that the major role of the ciliated protozoa in the activated-sludge process is to clarify the effluents. Indeed, evidence from surveys of full-scale plants indicate that when protozoa are not present the effluent obtained is turbid and of low quality. There are at least two ways in which protozoa might cause the improvement in effluent clarity; either by flocculation or by predation. There is a considerable amount of published evidence showing that pure cultures of protozoa can flocculate suspended particulate matter and bacteria. This can aid both clarification of the effluent and the formation of the sludge flocs. In some species flocculation is thought to be brought about by the secretion of a mucous-like substance from the oral area. However, there is also evidence to suggest two mechanisms from experiments with the ciliate *Paramecium caudatum* flocculating colloidal suspensions of Indian ink. Firstly, the ciliate secretes a soluble polysaccharide into the medium which changes the surface charge of the colloidal particles, and secondly, particles ingested during cyclosis are glued together by a mucin. However, protozoa may not be the cause of flocculation. Many bacteria are able to grow in flocculant forms or flocculate in the absence of protozoa.

It is evident that the vast majority of ciliates found in sewage-treatment processes feed mainly upon bacteria and so it has been suggested that the predatory activities of the protozoa might be responsible for the removal of bacteria from effluents. It has been shown that ciliates from activated-sludge plants can feed upon a whole variety of bacteria likely to be present, but until the mid-1960s there were no data on the quantitative aspects of protozoan feeding. Studies using batch and continuous-culture methods have now supplied sufficient data to be able to assess the quantities of bacteria likely to be removed by protozoa. It seems that the protozoa could, by predation alone, easily account for the removal of bacteria in the activated sludge of the experiments. Protozoa are known to feed upon pathogenic bacteria, including those which cause diseases such as diphtheria, cholera, typhus and streptococcal infections as well as faecal bacteria such as *Escherichia coli*. In the case of *E. coli* it has been found that, in the absence of protozoa, 50 per cent of the bacteria entering are removed by unidentified processes, but probably simple death. When ciliates are present about 95 per cent are removed.

It seems likely from such evidence that the major role of the ciliated protozoa in aerobic sewage-treatment processes is the removal of dispersed growths of bacteria by predation. It is unlikely that protozoa-induced flocculation is of any real importance. Flagellated protozoa and amoebae also feed upon bacteria and they, no doubt, play a similar role. Furthermore, the amoebae may also have the ability to ingest flocculated bacteria, which would have the effect of reducing sludge production. It is well known that protozoa are also able to utilise soluble substrates, but to date no work has been carried out on the quantitative aspects of substrate utilisation when the protozoa also have a plentiful supply of bacteria present as food.

7

Modelling microbial population dynamics

It is often difficult to predict how the different operating conditions of an activated-sludge plant might affect the microbial populations. Similarly it is difficult to understand the implications of microbial population change noted in full-scale plants. There are two ways of overcoming these difficulties, by experimentation and by mathematical modelling. Both methods have their advantages but it is the latter which forces a logical approach and stimulates the formulation of new experiments to provide necessary data. Neither method alone will supply all the answers and a healthy mixture of the two is usually the best approach. Mathematical models can be simulated on a computer so that dynamic solutions can be investigated visually.

It has already been shown that the activated-sludge process is a highly complicated biological system which relies upon the growth of organisms either to remove unacceptable compounds from sewage or to convert them into something more acceptable. In some cases we know which organisms carry particular steps in the process and a study of the growth kinetics of these organisms has led us to understand the process more fully and to predict the effect of changing operating parameters upon the growth of the organisms and hence upon effluent quality. The aim of this chapter is to lead the reader through the process of compiling a mathematical model of the activated-sludge process and thereby explain the basic rationale behind the dynamics of activated-sludge bacterial and ciliate populations.

Activated-sludge model

Before we can begin to consider organisms we must first consider the habitat. In this case it is an activated-sludge plant. An outline of the plant to be modelled is given in fig 7.1. It consists of a single completely

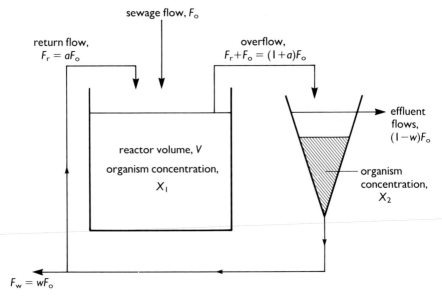

Fig 7.1 Outline of activated-sludge plant used in mathematical models illustrating flows to and from each part of the system.

mixed reactor or aeration vessel which has a volume V. Mixed liquor overflows from the reactor into a sedimentation tank where any organisms capable of doing so will settle to the bottom. Some of the settled sludge is returned back to the aeration vessel while some is continually wasted. It is a matter of convenience to express all flow rates in terms of the rate at which fresh sewage enters the reactor, i.e. the sewage flow rate, F_o, which is measured in units of volumes per hour. If the rate at which settled sludge is recycled back to the reactor is F_r, then we can express it in terms of sewage flow rate by use of the term a, the volume ratio of recycled sludge flow to sewage flow where:

$$a = F_r / F_o$$

This means that there are two flows, F_o and aF_o, both entering and leaving the reactor. If after sedimentation some of the flow, F_w, is diverted to waste, then this too can be expressed in terms of sewage flow rate by use of the term w, where:

$$w = F_w / F_o$$

The only flow remaining is that of effluent, F_e, which by simple algebra can be calculated to be equal to $(1 - w) F_o$.

Sewage-plant operators often refer to the length of time that sewage remains in the aeration tank as the sewage retention time (R). This can be determined by dividing the volume of the plant V by the sewage flow F_o, i.e. $R = V/F_o$ which is usually measured in hours. However, it will be seen later that since we will measure microbial population growth as a rate it is more appropriate to convert sewage retention time to dilution rate, D, where:

$$D = 1/R = F_o/V$$

which is measured in terms of hours^{-1}.

If we have a concentration of organisms X_1 in the aeration tank and this is concentrated to X_2 at the bottom of the sedimentation tank, then we can introduce and define the concentration factor b, where:

$$b = X_2/X_1$$

and $b > 1$. Clearly if $b = 1$ then there is no concentration since X_2 would equal X_1, and if $b < 1$ then the organisms would be floating rather than settling.

Microbial population growth kinetics

Having considered the habitat we can now begin to consider organisms and in particular how they grow. Most of the organisms in activated-sludge plants are micro-organisms of various types and they reproduce asexually by some form of binary fission. The organism grows until it reaches a certain size and then divides into two cells, each of which proceeds to grow before further division. This leads us to one way of measuring the growth of micro-organisms, the so-called doubling time which is the time taken under a defined set of environmental conditions for a population to double its size. An example of this is given in fig 7.2. It demonstrates the growth of a culture of bacteria from which samples were taken at hourly intervals. The population was then estimated by taking an optical density reading of the culture using a spectrophotometer. The log of the population is then plotted against time in order to get a linear relationship between the two. The doubling time can easily be measured from such a plot; one chooses any population size, doubles it and measures the time interval between the two readings. The time interval is the population doubling time, t_d, measured in hours or minutes. The doubling time can easily be converted into a rate, the specific growth rate μ, by using the equation:

$$\mu = \log_e 2 / t_d$$

The specific growth rate of an organism is equivalent to the fractional increase of the population per unit time and is measured in hours^{-1}. Thus it can be seen that the dilution rate of the aeration tank and the specific growth rate of an organism can be measured in the same units of reciprocal time.

The specific growth rate of an organism is influenced by a number of environmental properties, such as pH and temperature, but principally by the concentration of the limiting substrate present. In most cases the specific growth rate of an organism is related to the concentration of its

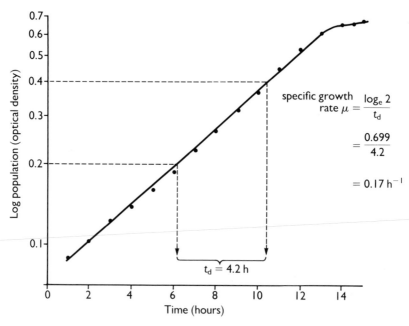

Fig 7.2 Graphical representation of the growth of a population of micro-organisms in a batch culture. The graph demonstrates how the doubling time, t_d, and specific growth rate, μ, may be calculated.

limiting substrate by the type of curve given in fig 7.3. This can be described mathematically by the Michaelis–Menten equation:

$$\mu = \frac{\mu_m\, s}{K_s + s}$$

where μ_m is the maximum specific growth rate, that is the rate obtained when substrate concentration, s, is in excess. K_s is the saturation constant and is numerically equal to the substrate concentration when $\mu = \mu_m/2$. Thus, provided we know the value of the kinetic constants μ_m and K_s, we can predict the specific growth rate of the organism at any particular substrate concentration and vice versa. There is an outline of a computer program in appendix 1 which can be used to simulate the growth of a micro-organism in cultures containing different concentrations of substrate. It can be used to estimate the kinetic constants of the organism.

In the case of bacteria the substrate is usually a soluble compound, perhaps a simple carbohydrate, and the equation fits experimental data very well indeed. However, in the case of bactivorous protozoa, the substrate is not soluble but a suspension of bacteria. In this case, although the equation is an adequate first approximation, the relationship between protozoan specific growth rate and bacterial concentration is not so simple as intraspecific competition has an effect. However, for the sake of

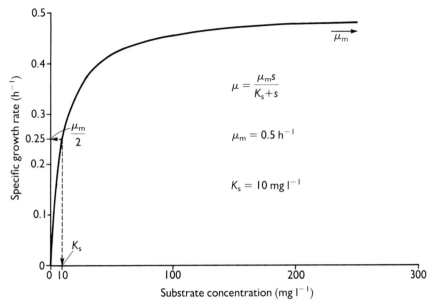

Fig 7.3 Graphical representation of the relationship between the specific growth rate of an organism and its substrate concentration.

simplicity it will be assumed that a simple relationship exists between the specific growth rate of a protozoan and the concentration of available bacteria according to the Michaelis–Menten equation:

$$\mu_c = \frac{\mu_{mc}B}{K_{sb} + B}$$

where B is the concentration of bacteria, μ_{mc} is the maximum specific growth rate when bacteria are in excess and K_{sb} is the saturation constant, numerically equal to the bacterial concentration when $\mu_c = \mu_{mc}/2$.

As an organism grows it utilises nutrient or substrate, and it has been shown that there is a simple relationship between the growth of an organism and its utilisation of substrate. As growth proceeds the concentration of substrate decreases and the growth rate is a constant fraction of the substrate utilisation rate which is termed the yield coefficient, Y. That is:

$$\text{Rate of change of organism concentration } X \text{ with respect to time } t \quad \propto \quad \text{Rate of change of substrate concentration } s \text{ with respect to time } t$$

or:

$$dX/dt = -Y\, ds/dt$$

The minus sign in front of the yield coefficient, Y, is necessary since the concentration of organisms is increasing (positive rate of change) whereas the substrate concentration is decreasing (negative rate of change).

Therefore it follows that over any finite period of time:

$$Y = \frac{\text{weight of organism formed}}{\text{weight of substrate consumed}}$$

Microbial populations

We can now consider the different types of microbial populations that may be found in activated-sludge plants and proceed to construct the equations necessary to describe a simple activated-sludge microbial community. It will be assumed that there are two fundamentally different bacterial populations; the first are sewage bacteria found at a concentration of 30 mg 1^{-1}. These remain as dispersed bacterial populations which do not flocculate and do not settle in the sedimentation tanks. This means that sewage bacteria can be consumed by any bactivorous protozoa present. The second bacterial population, the sludge bacteria, form the bulk of the sludge. They are not available as a food source for protozoan populations but settle in the sedimentation tank. Finally it is assumed that both bacterial populations will compete with each other for the soluble substrate in the sewage. This is, of course, an over-simplification of the real system but does have some basis in experimental observations. Bacteriologists have long known that the bacteria borne in sewage are different to those which grow in the plant and form the bulk of the sludge floc. Similarly it is known that ciliated protozoa do not have the necessary feeding structures to enable them to engulf large flocculated masses of bacteria.

Certain assumptions are also made about the protozoan populations. It is assumed that they are ciliates, which is normally the case. They may be of two basic types: either free-swimming forms which do not settle on sedimentation; or very closely associated with the sludge floc to which they are attached or crawl over its surfaces. In the latter case, as the sludge settles then the ciliates also settle. It is also assumed that ciliates are not present in sewage and that all types will feed upon dispersed populations of sewage bacteria. Table 7.1 summarises the assumptions made.

Mathematical models

We have now gathered sufficient information to write equations to describe the fate of different microbial populations in the aeration tank of the activated-sludge model illustrated in fig 7.1. In each case the different parts of the equation will be clearly labelled. A complete list of the notation used is shown in table 7.2.

Table 7.1. *Basic assumptions made about the microbial populations used in models.* ss = soluble substrate; sb = sewage bacteria

Organism type	Conc. in sewage (mg l^{-1})	Will it settle?	Nutrient used	μ_m (h^{-1})	K_s (mg l^{-1})
Sewage bacteria	30	no	ss	0.5	15
Sludge bacteria	0	yes	ss	0.3	10
Free-swimming ciliates	0	no	sb	0.35	12
Attached and crawling ciliates	0	yes	sb	0.35	12
Soluble substrate	200	—	—	—	—

Sludge bacteria

The rate of change of sludge concentration in the aeration tank with respect to time can be expressed mathematically as:

Rate of change = growth + recycled sludge − output

$$dX/dt = \mu_x X + DabX - DX(1+a)$$

where X and μ_x are the concentrations and specific growth rate (see page 83) of the sludge bacteria in the reactor respectively; D is the sewage dilution rate (page 83), a is the recycle ratio (page 82) and b is the concentration factor (page 83). It should be noted that the recycled sludge bacterial population is comprised of two parts, the recycle flow, Da (page 82) and the concentrated bacterial population bX (page 83). Output from the reactor includes both flow components, $D + aD$ (page 82). At steady state, by definition, the rate of change will be zero (i.e. $dX/dt = 0$) and the equation can be rearranged such that:

$$\mu_x = D + D(a - ab)$$

Since the concentration factor $b > 1$ (see page 82) then the term $D(a - ab)$ must always be negative so that μ_x must always be less than D. Thus at steady state the specific growth rate of an organism which settles is always less than the sewage dilution rate and this will be shown to be in sharp contrast with organisms which do not settle.

It should be noted that the specific growth rate is related to substrate concentration by the Michaelis–Menten equation (page 84):

$$\mu_x = \frac{\mu_{mx}\, s}{K_{sx} + s}$$

Table 7.2. *Notation used in mathematical models*

a	Volume ratio of recycled sludge flow to sewage flow (F_r/F_o)
b	Organism concentration factor (X_2/X_1)
B	Concentration of sewage bacteria in reactor (mg l^{-1})
B_o	Concentration of bacteria suspended in sewage (mg l^{-1})
C	Concentration of ciliates in reactor (mg l^{-1})
D	Sewage dilution rate (F_o/V) (volumes h^{-1})
F_e	Effluent flow rate (volumes h^{-1})
F_o	Sewage flow rate (volumes h^{-1})
F_r	Recycled sludge flow rate (volumes h^{-1})
F_w	Wasted sludge flow rate (volumes h^{-1})
H	Concentration of free-swimming ciliates in reactor (mg l^{-1})
K_s	Saturation constant (mg l^{-1})
K_{sb}	Saturation constant, sewage bacteria (mg l^{-1})
K_{sc}	Saturation constant, ciliates (mg l^{-1})
K_{sx}	Saturation constant, sludge bacteria (mg l^{-1})
P	Concentration of attached ciliates in reactor (mg l^{-1})
R	Sewage retention time (V/F_o)(h)
S_o	Concentration of limiting substrate in sewage (mg l^{-1})
s	Concentration of limiting substrate in reactor (mg l^{-1})
t_d	Doubling time of a population of organisms (h)
μ	Specific growth rate of an organism (h^{-1})
μ_b	Specific growth rate of sewage bacteria (h^{-1})
μ_c	Specific growth rate of a ciliate (h^{-1})
μ_h	Specific growth rate of a free-swimming ciliate (h^{-1})
μ_m	Maximum specific growth rate of an organism (h^{-1})
μ_p	Specific growth rate of an attached ciliate (h^{-1})
μ_{mb}	Maximum specific growth rate of sewage bacteria (h^{-1})
μ_{mc}	Maximum specific growth rate of a ciliate (h^{-1})
μ_{mx}	Maximum specific growth rate of sludge bacteria (h^{-1})
μ_x	Specific growth rate of sludge bacteria (h^{-1})
V	Volume of aeration tank
w	Wastage ratio (F_w/F_o)
X	Concentration of sludge bacteria in reactor (mg l^{-1})
X_1	Concentration of organisms in reactor (mg l^{-1})
X_2	Concentration of organisms in sedimentation tank (mg l^{-1})
Y	Yield coefficient (dimensionless)
Y_b	Yield coefficient of sewage bacteria (dimensionless)
Y_c	Yield coefficient of ciliates (dimensionless)
Y_x	Yield coefficient of sludge bacteria (dimensionless)

Sewage bacteria

The rate of change of sewage bacteria concentration in the aeration tank with respect to time can be expressed mathematically as:

Rate of change = input + recycle − output + growth − consumption

$$dB/dt = DB_o + DaB - (1+a)DB + \mu_b B - \mu_c C/Y_c$$

where B is the concentration of sewage bacteria in the reactor and B_o is the concentration in the sewage. The specific growth rates of sewage bacteria and ciliates are μ_b and μ_c respectively. The other symbols are as previously designated. A comparison of this equation with that for sludge bacteria will reveal that there are two extra terms, an input and a consumption. It should be remembered from earlier assumptions (page 87) that there is an input of bacteria in the sewage and that they are being removed by protozoan predation. It should also be noted that the recycled population term does not contain a concentration factor since sewage bacteria do not settle.

The specific growth rate of the sewage bacteria is related to substrate concentration by the familiar Michaelis–Menten equation:

$$\mu_b = \frac{\mu_{mb}\, s}{K_{sb} + s}$$

Substrate concentration

Since the growth rate of the organisms is controlled by the concentration of substrate then it is necessary to write equations for the fate of substrate in the reactor. The rate of change of substrate concentration in the aeration tank with respect to time can be expressed mathematically as:

$$\text{Rate of change} = \text{input} + \text{recycle} - \text{output} - \text{consumption}$$
$$ds/dt = DS_o + Das - (1+a)Ds - \mu_x X/Y_x - \mu_b B/Y_b$$

where S_o and s are the concentrations of soluble sewage substrate in the sewage flow and reactor respectively. Note there are two consumption terms due to the growth of sludge and sewage bacteria. The concentration of substrate in the reactor is very important since it determines the specific growth rate of the sludge bacteria. Furthermore, in a real plant it would be equivalent to the concentration of organic carbon leaving in the effluent and therefore contributing to effluent quality.

Ciliated protozoa

The two groups of protozoa have to be treated differently, depending on whether they settle or are free swimming. The rate of change of concentration of free-swimming ciliates in the aeration tank with respect to time can be expressed mathematically as:

$$\text{Rate of change} = \text{growth} + \text{recycle} - \text{output}$$
$$dH/dt = \mu_h H + DaH - (1+a)DH$$

where μ_h and H are the specific growth rate and population size of free-swimming ciliates respectively. It should be noted that there is no concentration factor in the recycle part of the equation since these ciliates do not settle and therefore do not concentrate. At steady state $dH/dt = 0$ and $\mu_h = D$, that is the specific growth rate of a free-swimming ciliate equals the dilution rate of the reactor.

The rate of change of sedentary ciliates can similarly be expressed as:

$$\text{Rate of change} = \text{growth} + \text{recycle} - \text{output}$$
$$dP/dt = \mu_p P \qquad + DabP \qquad - (1+a)DP$$

where μ_p and P are the specific growth rate and population size respectively. It should be noted that there is a concentration factor in the recycle term since sedentary ciliates attach themselves to sludge bacteria which settle. Comparison with the equation for sludge bacteria shows that they are in fact the same and, following the same argument used for that population, it can be shown that the specific growth rate of a sedentary ciliate is lower than the dilution rate of the reactor.

In both cases the specific growth rate of ciliates, μ_c, can be related to bacteria concentration by the Michaelis–Menten equation:

$$\mu_c = \frac{\mu_{mc}\, b}{K_{sc} + b}$$

Steady-state solutions to the model

So far we have described equations for the components of a model activated-sludge microbial community. The equations can be used to study the dynamic behaviour of the microbial populations and substrate concentration with respect to time (computer simulation). Simulations such as these demonstrate that the populations quickly approach stable (steady-state) values. Under these circumstances it becomes valid to solve the equations for steady-state values by making each equation equal to zero (i.e. rate of change equals zero). Fig 7.4 illustrates the steady-state values of the populations over a wide range of sludge wastage rates whilst keeping the sewage dilution rate arbitrarily ten times that of sludge wastage. The equations have been solved for three different situations: (A) when the protozoa present are of the sedentary type; (B) when the protozoa are free-swimming ciliates; and (C) when protozoa are not present. Calculations such as these enable the comparison of model predictions with the real observations from experimental and full-scale plants. Furthermore it allows one to explore the effect of changing the values of the kinetic constants, yield coefficients, etc. on the microbial populations and the effluent quality. A computer program is described in appendix 2 which enables steady-state solutions of the equations to be quickly calculated so that readers can carry out their own investigations.

It has already been shown (page 87) that the specific growth rate of settling organisms (sludge bacteria and sedentary protozoa) is less than the dilution rate at steady state, and equals the specific wastage rate of the sludge mass as a whole. In full-scale plants this would normally be about one-tenth of the dilution rate. This explains why in all three situations the substrate concentration is the same at any sludge wastage rate. The microbial populations, however, are different for each situation. The

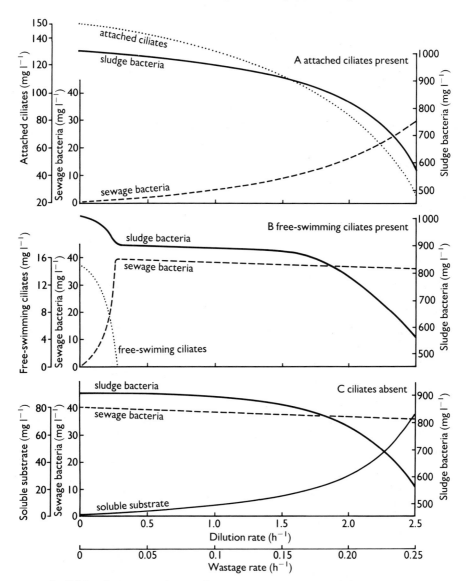

Fig 7.4 Steady-state populations of micro-organisms at various dilution and sludge wastage rates. A attached ciliates present, B free-swimming ciliates present, C ciliates absent. The substrate concentration curve in C was also obtained in A and B. From Curds (1971).

results in fig 7.4 show that substrate concentration is independent of ciliates. However, the turbidity of the effluent, due to dispersed sewage bacteria, is completely dependent upon protozoa. Large numbers of dispersed bacteria are present when protozoa are absent (no predation), but are fewer when free-swimming ciliates are present and least when the ciliate population is composed of sedentary forms. The first case is simple to explain; when there is no predation the sewage bacteria pass through the process without removal and can increase somewhat by growth. The latter two cases can also be explained; at steady state the growth rate of a free-swimming ciliate equals that of the dilution rate D, whereas that of a sedentary ciliate is lower than D and equal to the very much lower wastage rate. It follows from the Michaelis–Menten equation that higher growth rates require higher concentrations of substrate to be present, which in this case is dispersed sewage bacteria. Furthermore, free-swimming ciliates are washed out of the system at much lower dilution rates than sedentary ciliates because the former are not recycled back into the aeration tank.

From these theoretical considerations an overall high-quality effluent would be expected to be obtained when sedentary ciliates are dominant, a slightly worse effluent quality due to increased turbidity when free-swimming ciliates are present. These predictions from the mathematical models are borne out by practical experience. For example, in practice free-swimming ciliates and flagellates are frequently taken to indicate a low-efficiency plant and the peritrichous ciliates (all sedentary) are indicative of a high-efficiency one. Indeed indicator species studies often list the free-swimming ciliates as being those more frequently found in plants producing inferior effluents ($BOD_5 > 21$ mg l^{-1}) whereas sedentary species of the genera *Vorticella*, *Epistylis* and *Carchesium* are more commonly observed in plants producing good quality effluents ($BOD_5 < 20$ mg l^{-1}).

The presence of protozoa and the habit of the dominant species therefore directly influence the concentration of dispersed sewage bacteria present and hence, indirectly, the concentration of sludge bacteria since these two groups of bacteria are in direct competition for the soluble substrate. Thus the greater the concentration of sewage bacteria present, the smaller the population of sludge bacteria present.

Computer simulations of the model

It is relatively simple to simulate the dynamics of the activated-sludge model on a computer. It is a matter of providing some starting values for the populations and then integrating against time using the equations described earlier (pages 87–90). This enables one to predict the dynamic behaviour of the populations over a specified period of time which is quite different to obtaining steady-state solutions to the equations. However, when the existing equations are simulated, all populations begin to move towards their steady-state values. This is not what is found in full-scale plants; population sizes do not remain constant, they change daily, demonstrating that there is a difference between real data and those obtained from the model.

Obviously the model is either wrong or incomplete. Since the model predictions agree with many other observations it is worthwhile establishing if there are any obvious, or not so obvious, omissions or erroneous assumptions that have been made which cause the model to predict a steady state. The most obvious omission is that sewage flow, strength and

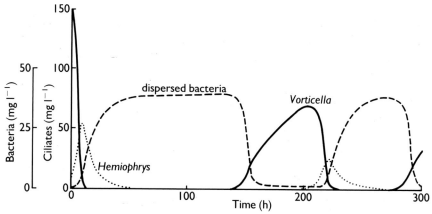

Fig 7.5 Effect of the introduction of the carnivorous ciliate *Hemiophrys*
into an otherwise stable activated-sludge microbial community. Sludge
bacteria and soluble substrate (not shown) also fluctuated. From Curds
(1973).

bacterial content are not constant throughout the day. It is well known that
the flow of sewage reaching a sewage works varies in a diurnal manner with
peak flows at midday and midnight resulting from the lag period following
increased toilet usage in the home, first thing in the morning and last thing
at night. Sewage strength varies in a similar manner and the little evidence
that we have suggests that this is also true for its bacterial content. If the
dilution rate, soluble substrate and sewage bacterial concentrations vary
sinusoidally, then oscillations are induced in all populations. On its own
each factor has little influence but together they have a summation effect
upon the populations and this will be reflected in a variable effluent quality.
That is an obvious example, but there is a less obvious one which stems
from the well-known dynamic behaviour which predators and their prey
exhibit. Many different examples in many habitats show that when a
predator and its prey are actively growing together then a common result is
that both populations oscillate in a repetitive manner. In activated sludge
some of the ciliates are carnivores feeding on other ciliates. Examples
include several free-swimming species such as *Hemiophrys* and *Litonotus*
which feed on attached ciliates such as *Vorticella* and *Carchesium*, and there
are the sedentary carnivorous suctorian ciliates which prey upon free-
swimming ciliates. If the model is rewritten to include a predator such as
one of these then regular oscillations are induced as shown in fig 7.5. The
predator/prey behaviour of the two ciliates induces oscillations in the
bacterial populations as the ciliate prey feeds upon the sewage bacteria.
Since the bacterial concentrations vary, then so does the effluent substrate
concentration. Because of these and other interactions that must be in
operation in reality it is easy to see why the microbial populations in a
full-scale plant do not reach steady states.

Earlier in this chapter it was shown that successions of protozoa are
obtained when an activated-sludge plant is started without the addition of a

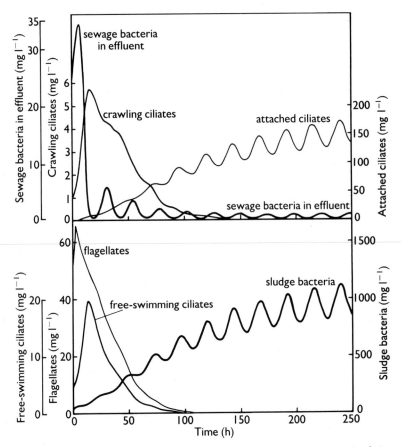

Fig 7.6 Effect of diurnal variations in sewage on the computer simulation of successions of micro-organisms during the establishment of an activated sludge. From Curds (1973).

sludge inoculum. The usual explanation given for these successions may be summarised as being due to changes in the environment which successively favour the growth of new types. Evidence and experience of computer simulations suggest that successions of this nature might equally well be explained simply on a basis of growth kinetics and the settling properties of the organisms. A computer program was written to describe the situation in a hypothetical activated-sludge reactor which contained sludge bacteria, dispersed sewage bacteria, flagellated protozoa, free-swimming ciliates and sedentary ciliates. Flagellates were not included before, but for the purposes of the simulation they were assumed to utilise the soluble substrate, would not settle and would not be present in the inflowing sewage.

Fig 7.6 illustrates the results of this simulation and demonstrates that the use of the above criteria gave a succession of organisms which was qualitatively similar to that found in reality. Flagellates and dispersed bacteria were the first dominant organisms, but as time progressed both declined. The flagellates declined slowly, owing to competition for substrate with the two bacteria, but the sewage bacteria declined rapidly owing to competition for substrate and the predatory activities of ciliates. The free-swimming ciliates reached a small peak after the dispersed bacteria but were soon displaced by the sedentary ciliates owing to competition for bacteria. The simulation showed that any organism which settles and is recycled back to the aeration tank has a distinct advantage over an organism which does not settle and is continually washed out in the effluent. If crawling ciliates are assumed to be inefficient sedentary forms then a peak of crawling ciliates should be expected to occur between the other two ciliate curves.

It would appear from these mathematical considerations that many of the observations made in the past concerning protozoa can be explained by the model. Although this is encouraging it does not necessarily mean that the model is correct. The activated-sludge community is highly complex and it is possible that the agreement of such simple models with reality is chance. The model was originally developed to explore how the populations might behave in a semi-quantitative manner and to lay the groundwork for a better understanding of the system. Since there are a very large number of possible permutations of reasonable values for the various constants and rates used in the equations there is still quite a lot of exploratory work to be done. It is hoped that the reader will take advantage of the computer program descriptions given in appendix 2 to carry out some investigations for him/herself.

8

Public health aspects

Not all protozoa are of value to the water industry. Some cause serious public health problems. Water engineers and public health microbiologists must be aware of these and be ready to act against them. Some, such as *Entamoeba histolytica*, the amoeba responsible for amoebic dysentery, are old adversaries, but in recent years others have risen to importance. Certain waterborne protozoan diseases such as amoebiasis, giardiasis and, recently, cryptosporidiosis are caused by true pathogenic parasitic protozoa which inhabit the human intestine and, in the encysted state, are transmitted from host to host in contaminated water. It is organisms from this group with which the general public are most familiar.

A second group which is generally unknown to the lay person comprises free-living pathogenic protozoa. These are all free-living amoebae which feed and multiply in water but can, given the right set of circumstances, invade humans with disastrous effects. Although the pathogenic free-living amoebae have only been known since the 1960s they have been responsible for the deaths of several thousands of people in that time by causing amoebic meningitis.

The third group of protozoa which give rise to public health concern are the least known of all. They too are free-living forms which harmlessly inhabit fresh waters but recent evidence has revealed that they can harbour pathogenic bacteria. They may be termed protozoan reservoirs of disease.

Pathogenic parasitic protozoa

There are three waterborne protozoan species which are human parasites. All three parasitise the human intestine and are distributed in water in the encysted state. The cyst will only hatch (excyst) inside the host. It serves only as a means of transmission from host to host since it can

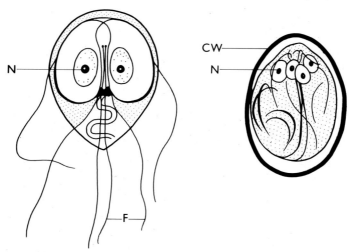

Fig 8.1 Diagram of *Giardia* and its cyst. N = nucleus, F = flagella, CW = cyst wall.

neither feed nor reproduce outside the human intestine. The three protozoa are the flagellate *Giardia lamblia* (producing the disease giardiasis), the amoeba *Entamoeba histolytica* (amoebic dysentery) and the sporozoan *Cryptosporidium* spp. (cryptosporidiosis). A fourth protozoan, the ciliate *Balantidium coli*, is also known to inhabit and cause disease in the human intestine. However, it is normally regarded to be a parasite of pigs and only occasionally infects humans. It too is transmitted from host to host in the encysted state but most human infections are restricted to farm workers in contact with pigs. Contaminated water supplies are not usually implicated.

Giardiasis – *Giardia lamblia*

Giardia lamblia is a flagellated protozoan which inhabits the human small intestine causing the disease giardiasis which has symptoms of stomach cramps, diarrhoea, nausea and fatigue. Giardiasis is endemic in many countries and *Giardia lamblia* has been identified as the causative organism in numerous outbreaks. The waterborne transmission of this organism was suggested as early as 1946 during an investigation of amoebiasis in a Tokyo apartment building. However, it was probably the reports of high incidences of giardiasis in American tourists visiting Leningrad in the 1970s which generally stimulated the recognition, investigation and reporting of the disease.

***Giardia lamblia* – the organism**   *Giardia* is a flagellated protozoan belonging to the class Zoomastigophorea. In appearance the trophozoite strongly resembles a child's kite (fig 8.1) since it possesses paired organelles and has bilateral symmetry. The anterior is broadly rounded and the body narrows towards the posterior so that it is approximately pear-shaped in outline. There are four pairs of backward-directed flagella and a pair of nuclei. A ventral disc (adhesive disc or sucker cup), located in the anterior half of the trophozoite, enables the parasite to attach to the walls of the intestine. Direct observations on living specimens have demonstrated that *Giardia* trophozoites can attach and detach themselves. When detached they swim by means of the flagella but even when attached they can also exhibit gliding and circling movements. It is presumed that attachment allows the parasite to maintain its position within the host during the peristaltic movements of the intestine. While there is still no general agreement on whether the trophozoites penetrate the intestinal mucosa, a body of evidence suggests that the trophozoites can sometimes invade the mucosa but do not progress beyond the ephithelial basement membrane.

Trophozoites reproduce in the host by longitudinal binary fission and fully grown trophozoites can encyst within the gut lumen and hence be voided in the host's faeces. In the life cycle of *Giardia*, it is the cyst which is the infective form and is solely responsible for the spread of the parasite to new hosts. Cysts are ellipsoidal in shape ranging in size from 6 to 10 μm (fig 8.1). Cysts can remain viable outside the host for several months depending upon the ambient temperature of the water, with survival times being longer at lower temperatures. Studies during the past decade have demonstrated that to excyst properly a temperature of 37°C is required. The process is induced by a pH of 0.5–2.0 followed by a pH of about 8.0 which mimics the pH changes in the human intestine.

Transmission   It was the frequent reports of American travellers to Leningrad in the 1970s contracting giardiasis from tap water which brought the disease to the public's attention. It was reported that 29 per cent of the personnel accompanying the US Olympic Boxing Team and 51 per cent of scientists visiting Leningrad conferences became ill at the end of the trip or shortly after return to their home countries. *Giardia lamblia* was isolated from faecal specimens from most of the patients in these groups. Russia is not the only country with a problem. Waterborne outbreaks are often reported in the United States and several outbreaks have been reported in the UK and other parts of Europe. In most cases the consumption of untreated or contaminated water appears to be the most important cause. Person-to-person transmission is relatively infrequent, as is contraction following swimming in unchlorinated pools or exposure to domestic animals. Interestingly eating raw vegetables has been implicated.

Hikers in certain parts of the USA frequently contract the disease by drinking from freshwater streams. These areas have sparse human habitation yet *Giardia* cysts and faecal coliform bacteria may usually be isolated from the streams. Several local wild animals, principally the beaver and sometimes the muskrat, have been implicated as the source but the case has not yet been completely proven. Certainly cysts of *Giardia* can be isolated from wild animal faeces but it is very difficult to distinguish *Giardia lamblia* from *G. duodenalis* and it could well be that the hikers are contaminating the mountain streams themselves.

The first waterborne outbreak of giardiasis involving a filtered water supply occurred in Camas, Washington where 10 per cent of the 6000 inhabitants were affected. *Giardia* cysts were isolated from the raw water entering the treatment plant as well as from treated water in two storage reservoirs. While the treatment plant met turbidity and coliform bacteria quality standards prior to the outbreak it was found that the chlorination plant had failed and several other deficiencies were found in the condition and operation of the filtration plant. Other outbreaks that have occurred since have usually been associated with design, operational or mechanical faults in plants. Originally *Giardia* cysts were thought to be highly resistant to chlorination but subsequent experimental work has indicated that the cysts are less resistant than was originally thought. Recent investigations have shown that the quality and temperature of the water are important parameters which must be taken into account when using chlorination to reduce the viability of the cysts. Higher temperatures and clear water are more effective at any given dose than cold, cloudy waters. Even so, the evidence is clear that the amount of chlorine required to kill *Giardia* cysts, especially at low temperatures, is considerably greater than that presently recommended for the treatment of water, which is aimed at the destruction of coliform bacteria.

Both physical and biological potable water filtration systems are effective in cyst removal. When rapid, that is physical, filtration systems are used it is essential that the filters are properly maintained and operated, preferably with a pre-treatment of chemical coagulation and sedimentation procedures.

Amoebic dysentery – *Entamoeba histolytica*

There are five species of amoebae which inhabit the human intestine. These are *Entamoeba histolytica*, *E. hartmanni*, *E. coli*, *Endolimax nana* and *Iodamoeba buetschlii*. In addition, *Entamoeba gingivalis* inhabits the mouth and upper pharynx of humans. Of these species only *Entamoeba histolytica* is pathogenic; the others are harmless commensals. *Entamoeba histolytica* usually lives as a commensal in the lumen of the large intestine (lumen amoebiasis), but may also invade the intestinal mucosa producing amoebic dysentery and secondarily invade extra-intestinal organs, mainly the liver, producing invasive amoebiasis. Clinically speaking, amoebic dysentery is an extremely well-known disease but biologically there are still misunderstandings associated with it which are largely derived from problems of species identification.

The parasite was discovered as long ago as 1875 but it was some years before the pathogenicity of *Entamoeba histolytica* was conclusively demonstrated. Even at the beginning it was noticed that there was more than one species of amoeba present in the large intestine and it was soon shown that while *Entamoeba histolytica* was pathogenic, the related species *E. coli* was non-pathogenic. As research work progressed it was realised that other harmless genera and species were also present and that *Entamoeba histolytica* was present in patients lacking the usual symptoms of dysentery and lesions. Furthermore, it was noted that invasive amoebiasis occurred in about 1 in 5 of infected patients in warm regions whereas in temperate zones infection was accompanied by clinical symptoms in only one in two million cases. The morphologically distinguishable related species *Entamoeba hartmanni* living in the human intestine probably accounts for many of the records from symptomless patients in temperate climates. This was for many years thought to be, and often referred to as, the 'small race' of *E. histolytica* but there is now conclusive taxonomic evidence for it to be regarded as a distinct and separate species. Species of the genus *Entamoeba* are classified on the basis of the number of nuclei in the mature cysts, where there can be eight, four or one. *Entamoeba coli* can easily be distinguished as it has eight nuclei and *E. polecki*, a common parasite of pigs but occasionally found in human hosts, has only one. However, the following five species all have four nuclei in the cyst: *Entamoeba histolytica*; *E. invadens*; *E. moshkovskii*; *E. hartmanni*; and *E. histolytica* Laredo-type. *Entamoeba invadens* is a parasite of reptiles and never found in humans. *E. moshkovskii* is a free-living amoeba that is not found in humans but is usually recorded from sewage and sewage-contaminated waters. *Entamoeba hartmanni* cysts may be distinguished from those of *E. histolytica* by their size. They are, on average, smaller than 10 µm (range 4–10.5; mean 7.4 µm) while those of *E. histolytica* are larger (range 9.5–15.5; mean 12 µm). *Entamoeba histolytica* Laredo-type amoebae are neither pathogenic nor morphologically distinguishable from *Entamoeba histolytica* proper. However, there are several differences between the two. These include the ability of *E. histolytica* Laredo-type to grow at temperatures below 37°C, to survive hypotonicity and have a distinct isoenzyme pattern, but they have yet to be divided into two distinct species.

Probably the two most puzzling aspects of the biology of *Entamoeba histolytica* are the, as yet, unexplained variability of its pathogenic potential and the restriction of human invasive amoebiasis to certain geographical regions of the world in spite of its worldwide distribution. Commonly the amoeba lives as a harmless commensal in the large intestine; feeding, growing and forming cysts without the patient showing any pathological effects. However, in areas such as Mexico, Western and South-east Asia and Southern Africa infection with *Entamoeba histolytica* is associated with the invasive form of the disease having symptoms of dysentery and liver abscesses.

Over the past 50 years or so three major theories have emerged in an attempt to answer this puzzle. The original theory was '*Entamoeba histolytica* is always a destroyer of tissue, but by no means always a producer of disease'. That is to say there can be a balance between host and parasite even though the latter is feeding on host tissues. This idea has now lost favour since it does not explain some of the geographical differences, nor do carriers without symptoms show evidence of intestinal invasion. The second theory states that there are two different but morphologically indistinguishable species of *Entamoeba histolytica*. This was based on epidemiological grounds and proposed that the species which is more prevalent in the warmer parts of the world causes the disease while another morphologically indistinguishable species was cosmopolitan in its distribution. This hypothesis initially only found support in France but more recently there has been renewed interest. The major evidence in its favour is that the enzyme patterns of the two strains of amoebae are different. This issue is important since it would indicate that only those patients harbouring pathogenic amoebae need be treated.

The final hypothesis, which has been prevalent in the literature for the last 20 years, proposed that there are several, but an unknown number of, strains with varying degrees of virulence. The most virulent ones are restricted to warmer climates, while those of lower virulence have a worldwide distribution. Even the newer biochemical methods of enzyme and total DNA analysis have not yet solved this taxonomic problem. Yet they have provided further evidence to support identification of some of the previously known morphological species. It seems likely that the problem will eventually be solved one way or another by the use of more sophisticated DNA methodology.

Morphology and life cycle *Entamoeba histolytica* exists in two forms as a trophozoite – a moving, feeding and dividing naked amoeba, and as a cyst. The cyst is the transmissive stage which does not develop further within the host but is voided in the faeces. It can survive outside the host for some time and, when swallowed by a susceptible host, passes unharmed through the stomach to excyst and emerge in the small intestine as an amoeba with four nuclei. The nuclei of the newly emerged amoeba divide to produce eight nuclei and this is followed by cytoplasmic division so that eight small uninucleate amoebae are produced. These enter the large intestine where they grow to full size. Healthy trophozoites move forward in a flowing motion reminiscent of the garden slug (*Limax* sp.). Hence this type of locomotion is usually referred to as 'limax-type movement'. In a temperature of 37 °C the whole body flows forward through a single, broad, anterior pseudopodium. At lower temperatures the amoeba shows signs of distress producing several pseudopodia simultaneously and then quickly withdrawing them.

The trophozoite contains a single nucleus. Food vacuoles containing bacteria and host cell nuclei may be seen in asymptomatic hosts, but red blood cells are seen in those of the amoebae which cause invasive amoebiasis. In the gut lumen the trophozoites are 10–20 µm in diameter but in the invasive phase in the gut mucosa, submucosa and liver they are larger (20–50 µm). Trophozoites will encyst only in the lumen of the host's intestine, never in the tissues. The trophozoite stops moving, rounds up and secretes a thin cyst wall. The nucleus undergoes two divisions to produce the characteristic four nuclei and the cyst is voided in the faeces.

Transmission   Faecal contamination of drinking water is a major source of transmission of amoebiasis, although food contamination is also important. Incidence of the disease is much higher in lower income groups, particularly where there are poor standards of personal hygiene, unprotected water supplies and primitive waste disposal. Defects in plumbing systems involving cross-connections between sewers and water supplies, back siphonage of toilets and leaking water pipes submerged in sewage have all been implicated in bringing *Entamoeba histolytica* cysts to the unsuspecting water consumer. The amoebae are usually found in low densities in sewage and become even fewer during treatment, presumably being settled out with the rest of the solids. They do not survive anaerobic digestion, particularly in heated anaerobic digesters, since cyst survival is reduced by 30 per cent for each 10°C rise in temperature. Survival experiments indicate that cysts of *Entamoeba histolytica* may persist in good quality water for up to 150 days but are sensitive to desiccation and temperatures above 50°C or below −5°C. The cysts have considerable resistance to chlorination but can be killed in drinking water by superchlorination. A residual chlorine concentration of 2–3 mg l^{-1} will kill over 99 per cent of the cysts in 20–30 minutes. However, this is influenced by the organic content of the water and, since water containing cysts is usually organically contaminated, greater quantities of chlorine are necessary.

It has been known for many years that rapid sand filtration removes 99.99 per cent of *Entamoeba histolytica* cysts. However, it was shown during the Second World War that these efficient removals do not occur in poor conditions of coagulation but that diatomaceous earth filters could essentially remove all cysts. As with the control of giardiasis, the usual recommended procedure for the safe control of amoebiasis is to use some form of sand filtration, with prior chemical coagulation, followed by chlorination.

Cryptosporidiosis – *Cryptosporidium*

Cryptosporidium is the only example of a waterborne coccidian parasite known to infect humans. *Cryptosporidium* infection has been described only in the last decade although it had been described from laboratory mice at the beginning of the century. In the early 1980s the onset of AIDS in the USA brought attention to the association of *Cryptosporidium* with diarrhoeal illness when 21 patients with both AIDS and cryptosporidiosis were reported to the Center for Disease Control. Prior to this only 11 cases, including four in immunologically healthy persons, had been noted in the world literature, and even a World Health Organisation report on parasite-related diarrhoeas did not include *Cryptosporidium* spp. Up to 1990 more than 110 patients with AIDS and cryptosporidiosis have been reported and at least 119 case reports have been published which present a much clearer picture of the epidemiology, clinical features, transmission and pathology of *Cryptosporidium* infection. Indeed the most recent evidence based on studies worldwide indicates that *Cryptosporidium* is the most common parasite found in patients suffering from diarrhoea.

Large-scale surveys of stool specimens from people suffering from gastrointestinal complaints indicate that, while *Cryptosporidium* is associated with diarrhoea in all parts of the world, it is most prevalent in the less developed regions. Prevalence in Europe was usually 1–2 per cent of those screened. In North America prevalence rates range from 0.6 to 4.3 per cent whereas in Asia, Australia, Africa and South America the rates reach 10–20 per cent. Duration and outcome of the disease vary considerably with the immunological health of the patient. In those suffering from AIDS, infections of long duration followed by death are most frequent whereas immunologically healthy people usually exhibit a shorter duration of symptoms (<20 days) and complete recovery. However, the cessation of diarrhoea does not indicate the end of infection since it has been found that patients excrete oocysts for a period approximately twice as long as they had diarrhoea. The site of *Cryptosporidium* infection is most usually the intestinal tract, particularly attached to the surface epithelial cells of villi and crypts of the small intestine. They have also been located in the stomach, appendix, colon and rectum.

Potential sources of infection include pets and farm animals, association with infected persons, international travel and contaminated waters. In the surveys that have been carried out many of the infected people had recently travelled extensively and in one group of infected travellers to the Caribbean a statistically significant association with the consumption of tap water was noted. Similarly infected households in San Antonio, Texas were served by a common, presumably contaminated, water supply. Such common-source outbreaks may result when *Cryptosporidium* oocysts escape filtration and are not susceptible to routinely used disinfectants. Several well-documented waterborne outbreaks of *Cryptosporidium* have now been reported. In Britain one outbreak in Reading was nationally reported over several days during 1989. Some outbreaks are believed to be the result of sewage contamination of drinking water sources but others have occurred after conventional treatments (coagulation, sedimentation, rapid sand filtration and disinfection) even though the turbidity and coliform bacteria standards were met. Waterborne transmission of enteric protozoa is obviously a major concern and the available evidence suggests that bacterial indicators (coliforms) of faecal pollution are not adequate in predicting the presence or absence of enteric protozoa. Because animals may serve as reservoirs of human infection, this type of contamination is now of major concern. The presence of protozoa in a potable water source necessitates that particular attention be placed on treatment for their removal or inactivation. As mentioned above, filtration has been recommended for all surface water supplies to ensure the removal of *Giardia* and *Entamoeba* cysts and parameters for the optimal cyst removal using routine filter systems have been investigated. However, no comparable data are yet available for the removal of oocysts of *Cryptosporidium*.

Pathogenic free-living protozoa

Over the last 20 years there has been an increased interest in the small free-living amoebae since *Naegleria fowleri* and various species of *Acanthamoeba* were found to be pathogenic and capable of causing fatal amoebic meningoencephalitis in humans and other mammals. These are the most recently discovered protozoa that can produce lethal effects upon humans and domestic animals. Until 1958, when their pathogenic potential in laboratory mice was first demonstrated, they were considered to be harmless, free-living amoebae of no particular interest to humans. Within a few years the first account of primary amoebic meningoencephalitis (PAM) was reported in humans. In fact, amoebic meningoencephalitis had been known for many years as one of the complications arising from invasive amoebiasis caused by *Entamoeba histolytica* whose primary locus is the intestine. However, PAM is different; unlike invasive *Entamoeba*, which secondarily affects the nervous system, the primary locus of this newly discovered disease is the central nervous system. Hence it is distinguished from amoebic meningoencephalitis by the addition of the word 'primary'.

It is now known that PAM is caused by *Naegleria fowleri* but there is a related disease called granulomatous amoebic encephalitis (GAE) which is caused by various species of the genus *Acanthamoeba*. Both organisms are capable of invading the brain and central nervous system but the latter species may also affect the lungs and skin in chronically ill patients and the eyes of healthy persons. Immediately after the first report of PAM in Australia there quickly followed reports of other human cases from Czechoslovakia and the USA. Since then other cases have been reported worldwide, including Britain, Belgium, Australia, New Zealand, Africa, India and South America, and by the end of 1983 about 160 cases had been confirmed.

Primary amoebic meningoencephalitis – *Naegleria fowleri*

Naegleria fowleri is a naturally occurring free-living amoeba. The trophozoite, or feeding and reproducing stage, is the amoeba which is active, variable in size and shape and characterised by blunt pseudopodia called lobopodia. When rounded the amoebae measure from about 8 to 30 μm in diameter. When moving in a single direction the amoeba is finger-like in shape but it quickly changes direction and several pseudo-podia may be produced. Like other amoebae the cytoplasm is finely granular and contains food vacuoles, a contractile vacuole and a conspic-uous nucleus. If suspended in distilled water *Naegleria* will develop from 2 to 9 temporary flagella whereas few other amoebae have a flagellated stage. Only amoebae belonging to the order Schizopyrenida have the ability to produce temporary flagella and members of the Amoebida, including *Acanthamoeba* spp., lack this ability. After about 24 hours the flagellated stage reverses to the amoeboid stage again. *Naegleria* also have the ability to survive desiccation for extended periods by secreting a cyst wall.

Naegleria fowleri is a thermophilic (heat-loving) amoeba which will grow well at temperatures up to 45°C and many reports of the disease have shown that it was contracted in swimming pools or artificial lakes in the summer months or near to the discharge outlets of power plants where elevated temperatures promote the growth of this species. Other outbreaks have taken place in hot springs in New Zealand, Australia and in the Roman baths at Bath, England. Though several of the European outbreaks were not associated with particularly high temperatures, in all cases the patient had swam recently in contaminated water. Naturally, as a thermophile, *Naegleria fowleri* has an advantage over other amoebae at warm temperatures but it is equally possible that the lower incidence of disease reported from cooler waters reflects human swimming behaviour rather than the absence of the pathogen. PAM always occurs in normal healthy individuals with a recent history of a water-related sporting activity. The disease is more common in the young and this is thought to be linked to their different behaviour in water. They are more likely to take contaminated waters up into the nose. The amoeba can then enter the body via the nasal mucosa and its nervous supply. From the nose the amoeba migrates to the brain, spinal cord and fluid. Symptoms usually start within 2–3 days of initial contact as severe headaches, stiff neck, fever and vomiting. Coma quickly follows and most cases have led to death within about a week of the appearance of the first symptoms.

Prevention of PAM is of prime importance in the control of the disease since once contracted a cure is unlikely to be successful. As most patients contract the disease in swimming pools, regular maintenance, including cleaning, filtration and chlorination, is strongly advocated. However, chlorination is not the complete solution since amoebae tend to be resistant to chlorine. Furthermore the presence of organic matter and bacteria increases the quantity of chlorine necessary to sterilise the water. After some outbreaks in Southern Australia, the South Australia Health Commission conducted a major campaign to bring the risks of swimming in contaminated water and the necessity of thorough and regular cleansing of home swimming pools to the notice of the general public. The control of organic matter and pollution are apparently of prime importance in prevention and although chlorination helps, it is not always effective against the pathogenic strains. Experimental work has demonstrated that 0.5 mg l^{-1} of free-chlorine residual at pH 7 is sufficient to kill about 99 per cent of the trophozoites within a period of 30 minutes. The disinfectant 'Baquacil' has been tested and proven to be effective. Swimming in lakes, rivers or swimming pools polluted by sewage and organic matter particularly should be avoided since this encourages the growth of bacteria and the amoebae which prey upon them.

Granulomatous amoebic encephalitis (GAE) – *Acanthamoeba* spp.

Unlike PAM which is an acute disease affecting previously healthy patients who have recently swum in water, GAE is a chronic disease preferentially affecting chronically sick patients, and immunologically compromised individuals who have not necessarily been exposed to contaminated waters. Like *Naegleria fowleri*, *Acanthamoeba* spp. are naturally occurring free-living amoebae. Those implicated in causing GAE include: *Acanthamoeba castellanii*; *A. culbertsoni*; *A. polyphaga*; *A. terricola*; *A. palestinensis*; and even a marine species, *A. griffini*. The trophozoites of these species are easily recognised and differentiated from *Naegleria* spp. by their possession of slender, spine-like pseudopodia. The trophozoite size range is slightly larger, from 20 to 40 μm. Otherwise the two genera are similar. When mounted on a slide they move in a similar manner but in *Acanthamoeba* spp. the edges of the body appears to be fringed. Unlike *Naegleria* spp., *Acanthamoeba* spp. do not have a flagellated stage but there is an encysted stage which is a response to desiccation. The cysts of *Acanthamoeba* spp. have a double wall which differs from those of *Naegleria* spp. *Acanthamoeba* spp. are not thermophilic like *Naegleria fowleri* and grow better at lower temperatures (25–30°C). *Acanthamoeba* spp. are widespread protozoans which can be isolated from the nasal mucosa of healthy individuals as well as from a wide variety of sources in nature including fresh water, air and soil. Infection preferentially attacks the chronically ill and immunologically compromised patients including some who have undergone immunosuppresive therapy. The disease GAE has rather different symptoms to PAM. Patients exhibit abnormal mental and behavioural changes, such as irritability, confusion, hallucinations and dizziness with seizures, fever and sometimes headaches. However, infection by *Acanthamoeba* spp. can result in a variety of diseases of which GAE involving the nervous system is only one. For example, some patients develop skin nodules a few days before the appearance of neurological symptoms. Also, *Acanthamoeba* spp. have been found to be responsible for certain diseases of the eye. Both *Acanthamoeba castellanii* and *A. polyphaga* have been implicated in causing chronic corneal ulceration that did not respond to anti-bacterial, -fungal or -viral treatments and in some cases blindness has resulted from the inflammation and ulceration. Unlike *Naegleria fowleri*, the source of infection by *Acanthamoeba* spp. is not limited to water. Entry of *Acanthamoeba* spp. into the body may be via the lower respiratory tract, ulcerations of the skin or mucosa or via other open wounds. This means that sensitive individuals can contract the disease from the air as well as from contaminated water. *Acanthamoeba* spp. are extremely resistant to drug treatment and so prevention is very important but even more difficult than with *Naegleria fowleri* since airborne cysts can be infective as well as waterborne trophozoites. As far as water is concerned, the precaution of maintaining recreational waters as free from organic matter as feasible is recommended, particularly as these amoebae are more resistant to chlorine than *Naegleria* spp.

Protozoan reservoirs of disease

The presence of bacteria in the cytoplasm of protozoa is well known and frequently reported in transmission electron-microscopy studies. However, most reports simply record their presence and assume some form of parasitic or mutualistic interaction between the two organisms. It is only recently that certain pathogenic bacteria have been shown to not only survive but also multiply in the cytoplasm of free-living, non-pathogenic protozoa. Indeed, it is now considered that protozoa are the natural habitat for certain pathogenic bacteria. To date the main focus of attention has been upon the bacterium *Legionella pneumophila*, the causative organism of Legionnaires' disease, which is most frequently contracted from contaminated water-cooling towers.

Legionellae are common inhabitants of natural waters but *Legionella pneumophila*, the bacterial species most frequently associated with Legionnaire's disease and Pontiac fever, was, at first, only obtained from purpose-built water systems. It was the introduction of specific fluorescent antibodies for the rapid detection of *Legionella pneumophila* in environmental samples which showed that this organism can frequently be detected in many different freshwater habitats, lakes and rivers besides air-conditioning cooling towers. However, while the organism seemed to be ubiquitous in its distribution it proved to be fastidious in its cultivation requirements and difficult to recover. For example, it was not possible to recover *Legionella* from samples of Rhine river water despite the occurrence of the disease in patients who had been exposed to it. Problems such as these led to the idea that *Legionella* might live in association with other freshwater organisms including cyanobacteria, algae and protozoa. Many of these organisms share identical freshwater habitats with *Legionella*. Observations of an apparent growth relationship between *Legionella* and blue-green algae in thermal environments led to several laboratory studies on these two organisms. It was found that *Legionella pneumophila* would indeed grow in pure cultures of cyanobacteria and algae. However, *Legionella pneumophila* can also be isolated from dark habitats where blue-green and green algae cannot survive.

The main host cells for legionellae in the human lung are the macrophages which are bactivorous amoeboid cells. Amoebae are usually found in environmental samples with legionellae. The amoebae are ubiquitous and can be isolated from potable water, water tanks, showers, humidifiers and cooling towers as well as from all natural water sources. Laboratory experiments have shown that as well as being ingested by amoebae, some *L. pneumophila* are attracted to the rear of the amoebae where they are taken into a vesicle. The bacteria reproduce within the vesicle which eventually almost entirely fills the cytoplasm of the amoeba. This bursts to release motile legionellae. The amoebae can encyst with legionellae-filled vesicles enabling both amoebae and bacteria to survive inferior environmental conditions including some chlorination. These experiments demonstrated that there was strong circumstantial evidence to implicate amoebae as natural hosts for legionellae and explains much of the epidemiology of Legionnaire's disease.

Circumstantial evidence is not sufficient to be certain that amoebae are acting as hosts in the natural environment. However, recent evidence from the Rhine has shown that the three freshwater amoebae *Acanthamoeba*, *Hartmanella* and *Naegleria* are frequently found in the river water. Also *Legionella* capable of causing disease in guinea pigs can be isolated from the amoebae. This is the first positive proof that *Legionella pneumophila* is found in naturally occurring amoebae and has important implications on the detection and control of the disease which can often be lethal to humans. Several microbiologists are of the opinion that this is not the only association of a pathogenic organism with protozoa. Laboratory studies have also shown that other protozoa, including the ciliates *Tetrahymena* and *Cyclidium*, can also act as host to legionellae so the phenomenon may be more widespread than was originally suspected.

Appendix I

Outline of computer program to simulate a laboratory study of microbial growth

Note Since BASIC varies between computers only an outline is given and it will be necessary to write the program for your own machine.

The program should be used to obtain microbial population growth rate data at different substrate concentrations. When the program is run you will be asked to supply starting concentrations for substrate and microbe. You will also be asked to choose the time interval at which you will sample the culture for microbial and substrate estimations. The model should be arranged to be as life-like as possible so that experimental problems commonly experienced will be encountered.

Estimation of doubling time

A set of microbe and substrate data will be obtained for each substrate starting concentration. The logs of the microbial and substrate concentrations should be plotted against time on a linear scale which will produce positive and negative linear relationships respectively. You should have included a random 5 per cent experimental error in measuring the microbial and substrate concentrations, in which case the line of best fit should be obtained by regression analysis. Doubling time should be converted into specific growth rate by use of the equation given in fig A1.1.

Estimation of yield constant

The yield coefficient is equal to amount of substrate consumed divided by the amount of organism grown over any finite period of time and this can be calculated from the growth and substrate curves (see fig A1.1).

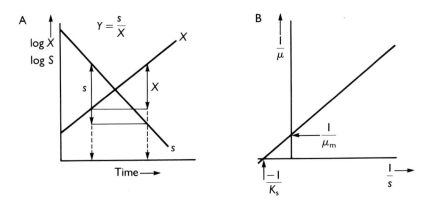

Fig A1.1 Estimation of microbial growth constants: A estimation of yield constant Y, B reciprocal plot used to estimate values of μ_m and K_s from microbial growth rate data.

Estimation of kinetic constants

After specific growth rates have been calculated for several different substrate starting concentrations these should be plotted on a reciprocal plot, i.e. $1/\mu$ against $1/s$ and the line of best fit calculated by regression analysis. The values of $1/K_s$ and $1/\mu_m$ may be obtained from the intercepts with abscissa and ordinate axes respectively (see fig A1.1).

Subprog 1   Set up arrays to accept calculated data; F1\$, F2\$ and F3\$ will be for time, organism and substrate concentrations respectively. Give values to the maximum growth rate UM, saturation constant KS, yield constant Y, and culture volume CV.

```
10 DIM F1$(20): DIM F2$(20): DIM F3$(20):REM***THESE ARE THE RESULT
ARRAYS
20 UM = 0.5: KS = 10: Y = 0.5: CV = 200
```

Subprog 2   Enter S1, the starting substrate concentration. Error traps should be included to ensure concentrations inputted lie within reasonable limits. If substrate is less than 5 or greater than 1000 then go to error messages saying starting concentrations are too low and too high respectively. When too high the student should be informed that they would have practical problems keeping the culture aerobic.

Subprog 3   Enter starting concentration of microbe, X1. Arrange error trap such that if X1 > (S * Y) then there is insufficient substrate to support the inoculum and student should try again.

Subprog 4   Enter sampling interval, T (decimal hours). Arrange error trap such that T > or = 0.1 and < 2.0 h.

Subprog 5   Get a random number, RN, between +1 and −1; calculate 5% of starting microbial population X1 and multiply this by RN. This will give a random error between + or −5% which can be added to X1.

Subprog 6

```
100  TM = 0: X = X1: S = S1: REM***TM, X AND S ARE THE CURRENT TIME AND
     MICROBE AND SUBSTRATE CONCENTRATIONS
110  CV = CV − 10: IF CV < 10 THEN M$ = "CULTURE RAN OUT": GOTO 400
120  U = UM * S / (KS + S): K = K + 1: REM***CONSTANT K USED TO INCREASE
     RESULT ARRAY ADDRESSES FOR EACH SAMPLE TAKEN
130  X2 = LOG (X) + (U * T): X2 = EXP (X2)
140  S2 = (X2 − X) / Y: S = S − S2: X = X2: TM = TM + T
150  IF S = < 0 THEN M$ = "SUBSTRATE RAN OUT": GOTO 400
160  REM*** ARRANGE THAT RANDOM 5% ERROR IS ADDED OR SUBTRACTED FROM X
     AND S TO MIMIC EXPERIMENTAL ERRORS. USE THESE VALUES FOR
     RESULTS BUT MAINTAIN ORIGINALS FOR NEXT CALCULATIONS.
170  REM** CONVERT RESULTS TO STRINGS IN PRINTABLE FORMAT INCLUDING
     NECESSARY SPACES: REM***STORE STRINGS IN RESULT ARRAYS
200  REM*** ARRANGE FOR TIME, MICROBE AND SUBSTRATE STRINGS TO BE
     PRINTED ON SCREEN
300  IF TM > 10 THEN M$ = "TIME RAN OUT": GOTO 400
310  GOTO 110
400  PRINT "EXPERIMENT OVER−": M$
```

Subprog 7   The operator should now be offered the choice to print the results on paper or end run.

Appendix 2

Outline of a computer program to calculate steady-state values of populations in mathematical models

This program is based on the mathematical model given in chapter 7 and can be used to generate steady-state values as illustrated in fig 7.4. Moreover, it can be used to explore the effects of operating parameters and values of microbial kinetic constants upon the populations and hence upon effluent quality. One useful exercise would be to attempt to produce the most efficient plant possible at any selected dilution rate; this should be done by changing the values of the kinetic constants. It should be remembered that an efficient plant is one which has a high effluent quality (low concentrations of sewage bacteria and soluble substrate) and yet produce as low populations of sludge bacteria as possible (since sludge bacteria also need to be disposed of by other processes).

Subprog 1 Set the default values of the 13 parameters

```
10 A = 1: CF = 1.9: MX = 0.3: KX = 15: MB = 0.5
20 KB = 10: MC = 0.35: KC = 12: YX = 0.5: YB = 0.5
30 YC = 0.5: B0 = 30: S0 = 200
```

Subprog 2 Ask if protozoa are present or not. If present $Z = 1$ and go to subprog 3, if not $Z = 0$ and go to subprog 4.

Subprog 3 Ask if protozoa are attached or free swimming. If attached $P = 0$, if free swimming $P = 1$.

Subprog 4 Print table of parameters on screen with ability to change their values.
Parameters are: Recycle ratio, A; Concentration factor, CF; Maximum specific growth rate sludge bacteria, MX; Maximum specific growth rate

112

sewage bacteria, MB; Saturation constant sludge bacteria, KX; Saturation constant sewage bacteria, KB; Maximum specific growth rate ciliates, MC; Maximum specific growth rate ciliates, KC; Yield constant sludge bacteria, YX; Yield constant sewage bacteria, YB; Yield constant ciliates, YC; Sewage bacteria concentration in sewage, BO; Substrate concentration in sewage, SO.

It should be noted that each input should have an error trap to ensure that new values fall between reasonable limits. These limits are given below.

A should be >0 and $=$ or < 1; CF should be < 2 and >1; MX, MB and MC should all be >0 and <1; KX, KB and KC should all be >1 and <100; YX, YB and YC should all be >0 and <1; BO should be >5 and <200; SO should be >50 and <1000.

Subprog 5 When parameters are set ask for dilution rate, D, to be input. D should be >0.

Subprog 6 The following equations should be used to calculate the results:

```
1000  UX = D * ((1 + A) - (A * CF))
1010  W = UX
1020  S = UX * KX / (MX - UX): IF S => SO OR S < 0 THEN GOTO 1600
1030  IF Z = 0 THEN GOTO 1100
1040  IF P = 1 THEN UC = D: GOTO 1060
1050  IF P = 0 THEN UC = UX
1060  B = UC * KC / (MC - UC): IF B => BO OR B < 0 THEN C = 0: GOSUB 1140:
      GOTO 1100
1070  UB = MB * S / (KB + S)
1080  C = (YC * D * (BO - B) + (YC * UB * B)) / UC
1090  X = (YX * D * (SO - S) / UX) - (YX * UB * B / YB * UX)
1095  REM*** GOTO subprog 7
1100  UB = MB * S / (KB + S)
1110  B = D * BO / (D - UB)
1120  X = (YX * D * (SO - S) / UX) - (YX * UB * B / YB * UX)
1130  REM*** GOTO subprog 7
1140  REM*** Write screen message telling operator that ciliates
      have  been washed out of the system but that calculations will
      continue. Your program will need to return to 1060.
1600  REM*** Write screen message telling operator that sludge has
      been washed out of system and calculations have been aborted.
      Your program will need to go to subprog  4.
```

Subprog 7 The steady-state values for the sludge bacteria, X, sewage bacteria, B, ciliates, C, and substrate concentration, S, have now all been calculated and the results should be made available either on screen or printed on paper. You may also wish to print or display the values of the 14 operational parameters used.

Subprog 8 Complete the program by giving the option of making further calculations or ending. If further calculations are required the program should be directed back to subprog 6.

Glossary

Abstracted water – water that has been taken from a natural source such as a river or groundwater supply.

Activated-sludge process – an aerobic sewage-treatment process by which settled sewage is treated biologically. The sewage is aerated using pumps, and solids (**activated sludge**) are removed by sedimentation. Some of the sludge is continually returned to the aeration tank after sedimentation.

Anaerobic digestion – a tertiary treatment process in which settled organic solids are fermented anaerobically. Methane gas is produced and the mass of solids is reduced considerably. The gas is often used as a source of energy.

Autotrophic – capable of synthesising organic compounds from simple inorganic ones. It includes those organisms which use sunlight as the source of energy (**photoautotrophs**) and those which obtain energy by the oxidation of inorganic substances (**chemotrophs**) such as sulphur, nitrogen or iron.

Biochemical oxygen demand (**BOD or BOD$_5$**) – the weight (mg) of oxygen consumed per unit volume (1) of a sample of water over a period of days at 20°C under a set of standard conditions. The oxygen consumed is due to the growth of micro-organisms on the degradable organic matter present.

Biodegradable – descriptive of a substance which can be broken down into smaller molecules by the action of microbes or other organisms.

Biological filter – an aerobic sewage-treatment process in which settled sewage is allowed to percolate or trickle over the microbial growth (film) which is attached to the surfaces of a bed of clinker or plastic. It is synonymous with the terms percolating filter and trickling filter.

Bulking – a problem encountered in the activated-sludge process. The

114

sludge is visibly light and fluffy so that it does not settle properly in the sedimentation tank. It can be caused by the unwanted growth of filamentous organisms in the aeration tank.

Chemical oxygen demand (COD) – the weight (mg) of oxygen consumed per unit volume (1) of a water sample following its oxidation by boiling with potassium dichromate and sulpuric acid for two hours. It is a measure of the concentration of chemically oxidisable organic material present in the sample.

Denitrification – a biochemical process by which many bacteria can anaerobically utilise nitrites and nitrates to produce nitrogen gas.
Dewater – to reduce the water concentration of a sludge or slurry, usually by means of evaporation.
Digestion – see anaerobic digestion.
Disinfection – the addition of chemicals, usually chlorine, to kill the micro-organisms present.

Effluent – a liquid, usually water, flowing from a plant or place. For example, sewage effluent is the purified water derived from sewage after treatment, and industrial effluent is waste water flowing from a factory.
Endogenous respiration – the consumption of oxygen by an organism utilising its cellular food reserves allowing it to survive but not to grow.
Epilimnion – a warm, less dense upper layer of water in a standing body of water (lakes, reservoirs, etc.).
Eutrophication – the formation of heavy blooms of green algae and blue-green algae in lakes following an input of nitrates and phosphates.

Heterotrophic – refers to organisms incapable of synthesising organic matter from inorganic substances but relying upon organic matter as a source of nourishment.
Holozoic – feeding in an animal-like manner by the ingestion of complex organic matter.
Hydrological cycle – the cycle of events through which water continually passes. Beginning as water vapour from the sea, it then condenses and precipitates as rain, to enter rivers and the sea again.
Hypolimnion – a cold, non-dense lower layer of water in a standing body of water (lakes, reservoirs, etc.).

Impounding reservoir – a very large reservoir usually constructed by building a dam across a river valley.

Maturation pond – a lagoon or pond used to polish an effluent after secondary biological treatment.
Micro-aerophilic – organisms with a preference to grow at very low dissolved oxygen concentrations.
Microstraining – the removal of suspended particulate matter from water using a fine-mesh metallic fabric filter. This is purely physical filtration and there is no improvement in chemical quality.

Nitrification – the biological oxidation of ammonia to nitrate. It is carried out in two steps by two different aerobic bacteria. Step one involves the oxidation of ammonia to nitrite (by *Nitrosomonas*) and step two by the further oxidation of nitrite to nitrate (by *Nitrobacter*).

Organic pollution – pollution by soluble or insoluble organic substances.
Oxidation pond or lagoon – an aerobic biological sewage-treatment process which relies upon photosynthetic algae to supply oxygen to the micro-organisms present.
Oxygen sag – the reduction in dissolved oxygen concentration in a river following the introduction of biodegradable substances.

Percolating filter – a term commonly used in the UK for a biological filter.
Phagotrophy – feeding by the ingestion of particulate organic matter.
Potable water – drinking water; water suitable for human consumption.
Primary treatment – the physical processes used at a sewage-treatment works to remove gross suspended solids prior to biological (secondary) treatment of the supernatant (settled sewage).
Pumped-storage reservoir – a reservoir built at the side of a river from which water is abstracted.

Rapid gravity filtration – the removal of suspended particulate matter from water by physical filtration through a bed of sand. Some improvement in chemical quality is also achieved.
Rapid sand filtration – a method used to produce drinking water. It involves the removal of suspended and some dissolved matter from the water by rapid flow (m h^{-1}) through a sand filter. The process does not depend on micro-organisms although there is always some improvement in chemical quality.
Reed bed – an aerobic biological sewage-treatment process which uses the reed *Phragmites*. The reeds keep the bed of soil or gravel partially aerobic by pumping atmospheric oxygen down to their roots. The micro-organisms in the soil carry out the purification processes.
Rhizosphere – the zone where plant roots are in intimate contact with the surrounding soil.
Rotating biological contactor (**RBC**) – an aerobic biological sewage-treatment process in which partially submerged vertical plastic or metal discs are rotated slowly in settled sewage. The discs supply surfaces upon which micro-organisms grow.
Roughing filtration – a physical (non-chemical) method to remove suspended matter and enhance the chemical quality of the water prior to slow sand filtration.
Royal Commission on Sewage Disposal – An independent body set up to advise Government on sewage-treatment methods. Replaced in 1970 by the Royal Commission on Environmental Pollution which has a wider brief.
Royal Commission standard effluent – a sample of water containing concentrations of BOD$_5$, ammonia and suspended solids equal to or less than 20:20:30 mg l^{-1} respectively.

Saprobic index – a numerical method of assessing river quality from the occurrence (and often abundance) of the species of organism present.

Saprobic system – a classification of river quality based on the species of organisms present.

Secondary treatment – the biological processes used in sewage-treatment works. They include biological filters, the activated sludge process, oxidation ponds, reed beds, etc.

Settled sewage – sewage which has had gross solids removed from it by screening and sedimentation. This is the physical (primary) treatment used before biological (secondary) treatment.

Slow sand filtration – a method used to produce drinking water. It involves the removal of suspended and dissolved matter from water by filtration through a bed of sand. The flow rate is always slow (50–300 mm h^{-1}) and the process depends upon the growth of micro-organisms which improve the water quality both chemically and physically.

Sludge digestion – see anaerobic digestion.

Suspended solids concentration – the concentration of solids in a sample of water as estimated by filtration through a glass-fibre filter paper.

Tertiary treatment – the processes, physical or biological, used in a sewage-treatment works following biological treatment. Tertiary processes include physical methods such as microstraining, or biological ones such as lagoons.

Thermocline – a narrow band of water separating the epilimnion and hypolimnion in a standing body of water (lakes, reservoirs, etc.). The water temperature and density rapidly change in this layer.

Total organic carbon (TOC) – the total concentration (mg l^{-1}) of organic carbon present in a sample.

Trickling filter – a term commonly used in the United States for a biological filter.

Bibliography

Adams, S.H. (1930). *Modern Sewage Disposal and Hygenics*. E. and F.N. Spon, London, 164 pp.

Arden, E. and Lockett, W.T. (1914a & b). Experiments on the oxidation of sewage without the aid of filters. *J.Soc.Chem.Ind.* **33**: 523–36; 1122–4.

Arden, E. and Lockett, W.T. (1915). The oxidation of sewage without the aid of filters. Pt 3. *J.Soc.Chem.Ind.* **34**: 937–43.

Bartsch, A.F. (1948). Biological aspects of stream pollution. *Sewage Works Journal* **20**: 292–302.

Caspers, H. and Karbe, L. (1966). Proposals for a biological classification of waters. *WHO-EBL-66.80* (Geneva), 1–28.

Clark, C. (1967). *Population Growth and Land Use*. Macmillan, London, 406 pp.

Clark, H.W. (1930). On the percolating filter. *Sewage Works Journal* **2**: 561–71.

Curds, C.R. (1971). Computer simulations of microbial population dynamics in the activated-sludge process. *Water Research* **5**: 1049–66.

Curds, C.R. (1973). A theoretical study of factors influencing the microbial population dynamics of the activated-sludge process – 1. *Water Research* **7**: 1269–84.

Curds, C.R. and Cockburn, A. (1970). Protozoa in biological sewage-treatment processes – I. A survey of the protozoan fauna of British percolating filters and activated-sludge plants. *Water Research* **4**: 225–36.

Curds, C.R. and Hawkes, H.A. (1975–83). *Ecological Aspects of Used-Water Treatment*. Vol. 1 *The organisms and their ecology* (1975), 414 pp. Vol. 2 *Biological activities and treatment processes* (1983), 308 pp. Vol. 3. *The processes and their ecology* (1983), 340 pp. Academic Press, London.

Curtis, E.J.C. and Curds, C.R. (1971). Sewage fungus in rivers in the United Kingdom: the slime community and its constituent organisms. *Water Research* **5**: 1147–59.

EEC (1982). *EC Directive relating to the Quality of Water Intended for Human Consumption* (80/778/EEC). Joint circular from DOE 20/82, 19 August 1982. London: HMSO.

Environmental Protection Agency (1976). *National Interim Primary Drinking Water Regulations*. Environmental Protection Agency, 570/9-76-003, p.34.

Fenchel, T. (1987). *Ecology of Protozoa*. Springer-Verlag, London, 197 pp.

Fjerdingstad, E. (1964). Pollution of streams estimated by benthal phytomicroorganisms. I. A saprobic system based on communities of organisms and ecological factors. *Internationale Revue der Gesamten Hydrobiologie* **49**: 63–131.

Gray, H.F. (1940). Sewerage in ancient and mediaeval times. *Sewage Works Journal* **12**: 939–46.

Hawkes, H.A. (1963). *The ecology of waste water treatment*. Pergamon Press, Oxford, 203 pp.

Hellawell, J.M. (1986). *Biological Indicators of Freshwater Pollution and Environmental Management*. Elsevier Applied Science Publishers, London & New York, 546 pp.

Holdgate, M.W. (1980). *A Perspective of Environmental Pollution*. Cambridge University Press, London, 278 pp.

Hynes, H.B.N. (1960). *The Biology of Polluted Waters*. Liverpool University Press, 202 pp.

Kalinin, G.P. and Bykov, V.D. (1969). The world's water resources, present and future. *Impact of Science on Technology* **19** (2): 135–50.

Kolkwitz, R. (1911). *Biologie des Trinkwassers, Abwassers und der Vortfluter*. In Rübner, Grüber, und Ficker's *Handbuch der Hygiene* II, 2. S. Herzel, Leipzig.

Kolkwitz, R. and Marsson, M. (1908). Ökologie der pflanzenlichen Saprobien. *Berichte der Deutschen Botanischen Gesellschaft* **26a**: 505–19.

Kolkwitz, R. and Marsson, M. (1909). Ökologie der tierischen Saprobien. Beiträge zur Lehre von der biologischen Gewässerbeurteilung. *Internationale Revue der Gesamten Hydrobiologie* **2**: 126–52.

Lee, J.J., Hutner, S.H. and Bovee, E.C. (1985). *An Illustrated Guide to the Protozoa*. Society of Protozoologists, Kansas, 629 pp.

Martinez, A.J. (1985). *Free-Living amebas: natural history, prevention, diagnosis, pathology and treatment of disease*. CRC Press, Boca Raton, Florida, 156 pp.

Metcalf, L. and Eddy, H.P. (1930). *Sewerage and Sewage Disposal*. 2nd edition. McGraw-Hill Book Company, Inc., New York and London, 783 pp.

Patrick, R. (1949). A proposed biological measure of stream conditions, based on a survey of the Conestaga basin, Lancaster County, Pennsylvania. *Proceedings of the National Academy of Science, Philadelphia* **101**: 277–341.

Patrick, R. (1954). The diatom flora of Bethany Bog. *Journal of Protozoology* **1**: 34–7.

Ravera, O. (1979). *Biological Aspects of Freshwater Pollution*. Commission of the European Communities by Pergamon Press, 214 pp.

Robins, F.W. (1946). *The story of water supply*. Oxford University Press, 207 pp.

Sladecek, V. (1969). The measures of saprobity. *Verhandlungen der Internationalen Vereinigung für Limnologie, Stuttgart* **17**: 546–59.

Suter, R. (1922). *Stream Pollution Studies*. State of New York Conservation Commission, Albany N.Y. 3–7.

Taylor, E.W. (1958). In *Examination of waters and water supplies*. Churchill, London, 513 pp.

Warren, C.E. (1971). *Biology and Water Pollution Control*. W.B. Saunders & Co, Philadelphia, London and Toronto, 434 pp.

Whipple, G.C. (1927). *The microscopy of drinking water*. 4th edition. Revised by Fair, G.M. and Whipple, M.C. John Wiley & Sons, Inc., New York, 586 pp.

Wood, L.B. (1982). *The Restoration of the Tidal Thames*. Adam Hilger Ltd, Bristol, 202 pp.

Zelinka, M. and Marvan, P. (1961). Zur Präzisierrung der biologischen Klassifikation der Reinheit fliessender Gewasser. *Archiv für Hydrobiologie* **57**: 389–407.

Index

121